Local Economic Development

Strategies for a Changing Economy

Edited by
R. Scott Fosler

PRACTICAL MANAGEMENT SERIES
Barbara H. Moore, Editor

Local Economic Development
Balanced Growth
Capital Financing Strategies for Local Governments
Capital Projects
Creative Personnel Practices
Current Issues in Leisure Services
The Entrepreneur in Local Government
Ethical Insight, Ethical Action
Hazardous Materials, Hazardous Waste
Human Services on a Limited Budget
Long-Term Financial Planning
Managing for Tomorrow
Managing New Technologies
Pay and Benefits
Performance Evaluation
Personnel Practices for the '90s
Police Management Today
Police Practice in the '90s
Practical Financial Management
Productivity Improvement Techniques
Risk Management Today
Shaping the Local Economy
Successful Negotiating in Local Government
Telecommunications for Local Government

The Practical Management Series is devoted to the
presentation of information and ideas from diverse
sources. The views expressed in this book are those of
the contributors and are not necessarily those of ICMA.

Library of Congress Cataloging-in-Publication Data

Local economic development : strategies for a changing economy /
    edited by R. Scott Fosler.
        p.   cm. — (Practical management series)
        ISBN 0-87326-085-6
        1. United States—Economic policy—1981- 2. Community
development—United States.   I. Fosler, R. Scott.
II. Series.
HC106.8.L63   1991
338.973—dc20   91-3830
                                                    CIP

Printed in the United States of America.
969594939291
54321

Local Economic Development:
Strategies for a
Changing Economy

The International City Management Association is the professional and educational organization for chief appointed management executives in local government. The purposes of ICMA are to enhance the quality of local government and to nurture and assist professional local government administrators in the United States and other countries. In furtherance of its mission, ICMA develops and disseminates new approaches to management through training programs, information services, and publications.

Managers, carrying a wide range of titles, serve cities, towns, counties, councils of governments, and state/provincial associations of local governments in all parts of the United States and Canada. These managers serve at the direction of elected councils and governing boards. ICMA serves these managers and local governments through many programs that aim at improving the manager's professional competence and strengthening the quality of all local governments.

The International City Management Association was founded in 1914; adopted its City Management Code of Ethics in 1924; and established its Institute for Training in Municipal Administration in 1934. The Institute, in turn, provided the basis for the Municipal Management Series, generally termed the "ICMA Green Books."

ICMA's interests and activities include public management education; standards of ethics for members; the *Municipal Year Book* and other data services; urban research; and newsletters, the monthly magazine *Public Management,* and other publications. ICMA's efforts for the improvement of local government management—as represented by this book—are offered for all local governments and educational institutions.

Foreword

During the past fifty years, government at every level has launched
or supported a range of programs in the name of economic development: industrial recruitment, urban renewal, downtown revitalization, "incubators," enterprise zones, and "grow-your-own" development, to name just a few. Although these efforts to fortify the
economy have their strengths, evolving global economic forces require a fundamental rethinking of the goals, methods, and assumptions of economic development.

Local governments must take the lead in developing new definitions of economic development and new strategies for achieving
it. Federal grants to assist with local development are becoming
more and more rare, and state efforts are often limited by the state's
own economic difficulties. Although it may seem paradoxical, the
globalization of the economy has made the local role more important
than ever. As Scott Fosler notes in his introduction to this volume,
"In a highly competitive economy . . . small actions matter." Local
governments are in an ideal position to take "small"—but potentially decisive—actions.

Local officials can provide the long-term, strategic vision that
successful economic development requires. They can manage government functions and services in ways that strengthen the local
economy. And they can work with education, labor, business, and
other groups to strengthen human resources, the application of
technology, enterprise development, and physical infrastructure—
just a few of the foundations on which economic development depends.

This book is part of ICMA's Practical Management Series,
which is devoted to serving local officials' needs for timely information on current issues and problems.

We are grateful to Scott Fosler for compiling the volume, to
Sandy Chizinsky Leas for her editorial guidance, and to the individuals and organizations that granted ICMA permission to reprint
their material.

William H. Hansell, Jr.
Executive Director
ICMA

About the Editor

R. Scott Fosler is Vice President and Director of Governmental Studies for the Committee for Economic Development (CED), a public policy research organization of 250 top corporate executives and university presidents. Mr. Fosler has directed the development of two CED policy statements, *Leadership for Dynamic State Economies* and *Public-Private Partnership: An Opportunity for Urban Communities*. Other CED projects he has directed include those on workforce investment, human resource policy, demographic policy, and public personnel management.

Mr. Fosler is a former municipal and county council member and served as president of the Washington Metropolitan Area Council of Governments, chairman of the Washington Area Economic Development Advisory Board, and chairman of the National Association of Counties' Steering Committee on Intergovernmental Affairs.

A graduate of Dickinson College, Mr. Fosler holds an M.P.A. from Princeton's Woodrow Wilson School of Public Affairs. He is a fellow of the National Academy of Public Administration, a senior fellow of the Johns Hopkins Institute for Policy Studies, and serves on the boards of the Public Administration Service and National Civic League. Mr. Fosler is the editor of *The New Economic Role of American States* (Oxford 1988) and co-editor of *Public-Private Partnership in American Cities* (Lexington 1982).

About the Authors

Unless otherwise noted, the following affiliations are those of the authors at the time of writing.

Edward J. Blakely, professor and chair, Department of City and Regional Planning, University of California, Berkeley.

Terry F. Buss, professor, Department of Urban Studies, the University of Akron (current affiliation).

Peter F. Drucker, Clarke Professor of Social Science and Management, Claremont Graduate School, California.

Mark Fall, Research Associate, State Policy Center, The Urban Institute, Washington, D.C. (current affiliation).

Robert E. Friedman, chairman of the board, Corporation For Enterprise Development, Washington, D.C.

C. Richard Hatch, Director, Center for Urban Reindustrialization Studies, New Jersey Institute of Technology, Englewood, New Jersey.

Harry P. Hatry, Director, State and Local Government Research Program, State Policy Center, The Urban Institute, Washington, D.C. (current affiliation).

James W. Hughes, professor, Department of Urban Planning and Policy Development, Rutgers University, New Brunswick, New Jersey (current affiliation).

David R. Kolzow, vice president, Greater Tucson Economic Council (current affiliation).

E. Blaine Liner, Director, State Policy Center, The Urban Institute, Washington, D.C. (current affiliation).

William E. Nothdurft, writer and independent consultant specializing in economic development policy (current affiliation).

David Osborne, author, *Laboratories of Democracy* (Boston: Harvard Business School Press, 1988).

Neal R. Peirce, author of the first nationally syndicated column on state and local affairs; the column is syndicated by the Washington Post Writers' Group (current affiliation).

Walter H. Plosila, President, Montgomery High-Technology Council, Inc., Rockville, Maryland.

Doug Ross, President, Corporation For Enterprise Development, Washington, D.C.

Thomas O. Singer, Research Associate, State Policy Center, The Urban Institute, Washington, D.C. (current affiliation).

Carol F. Steinbach, journalist specializing in housing and community development; contributing editor, *National Journal* (current affiliation).

George Sternlieb, director, Center for Urban Policy Research, and professor, Department of Urban Planning and Policy Development, Rutgers University, New Brunswick, New Jersey.

Roger J. Vaughan, Roger J. Vaughan and Associates, Santa Fe, New Mexico (current affiliation).

Robert R. Weaver, Executive Director, Concho Valley Council of Governments, San Angelo, Texas (current affiliation).

Contents

Introduction

R. Scott Fosler

The global economic revolution presents local economic development policy with four major challenges: to rethink the goals and assumptions of economic development; to strengthen economic foundations; to adapt to shifting geographical realities; and to create new organizational and institutional approaches to local development goals.

The first challenge requires local leaders to rethink the goals and basic assumptions of economic development in light of powerful forces that are restructuring the economy at all levels—global, national, state, regional, and local.

Economic development at the local level used to be equated with industrial recruitment, or "smokestack chasing," the practice of using financial inducements to persuade firms to relocate to a jurisdiction. Most local governments have expanded that focus to include business retention and new business startup, but many still see economic development as something that government "does," a function, like police protection or waste management, that can be assigned to an agency to "carry out."

Recently, however, many local leaders have come to view economic development not as a *function* but as a process rooted in the private sector. Local governments cannot "do" economic development. But the actions they take—or fail to take—in a wide range of areas over which they have some influence can affect the process of economic development in the private sector within their own jurisdictions.

This new view requires a sharpening of economic goals. It is no longer enough just to attract firms and create jobs—it also matters whether those jobs are associated with high skills and high pay in high-performance businesses, whether those businesses operate productively and competitively, whether economic vitality contributes to a jurisdiction's standard of living and quality of life, and whether the community has the capacity to sustain its economic productivity and competitiveness over time.

The second challenge is to strengthen the economic foundations and dynamics required to achieve local development goals. Local governments must develop a strategic vision of how they and other public institutions can motivate and support the private sector to promote economic vitality. This encompasses a wide range of public actions that affect the basic economic foundations on which the private sector depends—e.g., the workforce, knowledge and technology, financial capital, and physical infrastructure. Public motivation and support also involves the integration of resources to address the real needs of firms and clusters of firms.

The third challenge to local economic development policy is to adapt to shifting geographical realities. The new economy may be global in scope, but important economic functions continue to be conducted in regions. The economic vitality of a local jurisdiction depends on both the overall health of the region of which it is a part and on its own geographical location within that region.

The fourth challenge is to create new organizational and institutional approaches that will accommodate both a broader strategic vision and market-driven action. Viewed as a process rooted in the private sector and affected by a wide range of public-sector actions, economic development becomes a central concern not just of economic development specialists but of local policy makers and managers as well as private-sector and civic leaders. Successful economic development requires a wide spectrum of public and private institutions—government agencies, businesses, labor organizations, educational organizations, nonprofit institutions, civic organizations, and individual citizens—to improve their own performance and work more effectively with one another.

The articles in this volume address each of these four challenges.

Changing perspectives on local economic development

To put these challenges in context, it is helpful to understand why "local economic development" was traditionally associated so closely with the business attraction model and why it now encompasses much broader concerns.

The conventional view

In the decades following World War II, concerns about local economic development were dwarfed by the powerful momentum of national economic growth. The American economy was booming, with large national corporations mass-producing standardized products for a domestic market that was virtually free of foreign competition.

Exporting for such firms was relatively easy: the war-torn economies of Europe and Asia had little alternative but to buy American products designed for the American market.

In this environment, few local governments worried about economic development, which was seen as more or less automatic and inevitable. Most expected to simply move up the escalator, propelled by national economic growth.

Concern about local economic development in the 1950s and 1960s was confined principally to those regions and localities considered to be outside the mainstream of national economic growth. These included the South and Appalachia, neither of which had experienced the rate of economic growth that characterized the national industrial economy. Also included were the central cities of the Northeast and Midwest, which had once been in the forefront of national growth but were falling behind—at first because of suburbanization and later because of the weakening of their industrial base.

From a national perspective, local economic development was viewed as peripheral to the central concern with promoting national economic growth with price stability. These national goals were to be achieved principally through the use of such macro-economic tools as fiscal, monetary, and trade policy, all of which were the exclusive preserve of the federal government. Although debate has raged among various schools of macro-economic theory since the Second World War—neoclassical, Keynesian, monetarist, rational expectations, and "supply-side"—nearly all the contending schools have viewed the national economy as the basic unit of economic geography and held economic policy to be more or less the exclusive purview of the federal government.

In short, "local economic development" during these years was viewed at the national, state, and local levels principally as an exercise in helping distressed areas either to catch up with or to keep from falling behind the national economy.

A few federal initiatives have addressed the problem of distressed areas, such as the Tennessee Valley Authority, the Appalachian Regional Commission, the Economic Development Administration, and the Department of Housing and Urban Development. Other federal initiatives, including many of the Great Society programs, focused more on helping disadvantaged populations, especially the poor. But all such efforts have been peripheral to the mainstream economic interest of the federal government: to promote a macro-economic policy that is designed to keep the national economy as a whole on a path of steady growth with stable prices.

At the state and local levels, the primary strategy for distressed areas was not so much to build their capacity for wealth creation and "value added" innovation as to capture as much business as possible from other localities, principally through industrial recruitment. The South's pioneering efforts in "smokestack chasing," dating back to Mississippi's Balance Agriculture with Industry Act of the 1930s, seemed to have the desired effect of attracting manufacturing branch plants from the industrial North. However, many local governments in the South thereby locked themselves into dependence on low-wage manufacturing plants, many of which have since moved on in search of still cheaper labor abroad—without leaving a legacy of transferable skills, entrepreneurship, or enhanced tax base in the communities they abandoned.

Nonetheless, industrial recruitment, or business attraction, became the dominant model for regional and local economic development, spreading throughout the country as an increasing number of state and local governments viewed themselves as being in distress or in competition with other jurisdictions.

The shift in view

Until the 1970s, the conventional industrial recruitment model prevailed at the state level. But in the seventies, powerful forces of global economic restructuring began to compel states to rethink the assumptions underlying their approach to economic development.

New England, the first region to be hit with the full impact of global economic change, was also the first to experiment with new approaches that focused on internal development (variously termed indigenous, homegrown, grow-your-own, and grow-from-within development). These approaches were designed to increase access to financial capital, to commercialize technology, to improve the skills of the workforce, to promote exports, and to improve the general economic infrastructure. The movement spread to the Midwest during the recessions of the early 1980s and has since been adopted in some form by nearly every state.

In the meantime, the local economic development policies of many local governments also expanded beyond the narrow focus on business attraction to a more "entrepreneurial" concern with overall economic vitality. Indeed, many of the industrial cities of the Northeast and Midwest had launched their own brand of internal development early in the postwar years. With the Allegheny Conference on Community Development, for example, Pittsburgh pioneered the development of a public-private partnership to address issues such as flooding and smoke pollution, which were impeding the city's economic progress. In Baltimore, local officials worked with local business leaders on the Greater Baltimore Committee to revitalize the inner harbor. During the past two decades, efforts such as Richmond Renaissance, the Newark Collaborative, and St. Paul's "entrepreneurial city" have reflected a broadening view of economic development with greater participation by business and civic groups in the formulation and implementation of strategy.

Business attraction certainly has not been abandoned. It is still viewed as a necessity for hardship communities—especially small ones—that have no base for "growing their own" enterprise and are desperately in need of jobs for unemployed workers unwilling to search for employment in more economically prosperous regions. Moreover, business attraction has lost little of its political allure: a firm's announcement of its intention to relocate to a jurisdiction and bring a specified number of jobs remains a highly visible and newsworthy event.

But for most jurisdictions, attraction is but a part of a broader policy framework that includes business retention, startup, and modernization. The focus of recruitment, moreover, has tended to shift from a preoccupation with manufacturing branch plants or even businesses per se, to a more selective interest in economic resources—such as skilled workers, venture capital expertise, or firms that will strengthen local enterprise clusters—in order to fill gaps, complement the local economic base, or build on perceived strengths. Some jurisdictions also have become more analytical in assessing the relative costs and benefits of recruitment targets and the price they must pay to lure them.

The 1990s

As a result of the trends outlined in the preceding sections, responsibility for economic policy has shifted from the federal to the state and local levels and from government-stimulated recruitment and job creation to joint public-private initiatives geared to improving the process of economic development and a jurisdiction's capacity to support it. In sharp contrast to the period when the national economy was undergoing rapid growth, today's concern about local economic development is not confined to jurisdictions outside the American economic mainstream. In today's economy, every state and local jurisdiction needs to strengthen its economy's ability to create value, improve productivity, and compete in world markets.

This new, general responsibility for economic development is all the more compelling because despite a decade of growth in the 1980s, the United States entered the 1990s in recession and confronting major structural weaknesses. The federal budget deficit had pushed the national debt to more than two trillion dollars, absorbing about 15 percent of the federal budget for debt payment. The chronic trade deficit had made the United States a foreign debtor to the tune of five hundred billion dollars, projected to increase to one trillion dollars by the mid 1990s even with dramatic improvement. The new decade also found deteriorating physical infrastructure, an inadequately prepared workforce, weakness in financial institutions, and widely uneven economic performance among regions and localities as well as among economic classes.

Although local economic development should not be viewed as an exclusively local responsibility, it can be said that local actions now matter more than ever.

The federal government is pervasively involved in areas that are of critical importance to national, regional, and local economic development—areas such as technology, financial capital, human resources, and industry-specific regulation. But these are rarely acknowledged as being part of the national economic policy model. So the federal government continues to pursue a vast agenda of microeconomic actions under different guises—tax policy, budget decisions, defense procurement, regulation, trade policy, science, agriculture, finance, transportation, and energy, among others—without any coherent theory or policy framework against which policy in these areas could be tested or through which it could be integrated.

Federal policies in all these areas, in turn, have important regional and local economic development impacts. But the geographic implications are never considered in a cohesive manner, and indeed are rarely acknowledged as an aspect of the national economic policy model.

Meanwhile, chronic federal budget deficits have largely immobilized federal fiscal policy, and an enormous strain has been placed on monetary policy to guide the national economy between the extremes of inflationary and recessionary tendencies without distorting the international value of the dollar or undermining the ability of the United States to attract foreign capital.

Finally, federal grants to states and localities, many of which have addressed such economically important functions as human resources and physical infrastructure, have been shrinking for more than a decade. The practical consequence is that federal policy toward regional and local economic development has been left to the vicissitudes of ad hoc political competition in the Congress and executive agencies: states, municipalities, and counties simply vie for whatever federal favors they can get.

The states have been far more forthright than the federal government in recognizing the need for a new economic policy model, but success at the state level is uneven: state leaders struggle with many of the same economic problems that confront local governments. Indeed, one of the principal challenges facing both state and local governments is to learn how to work more effectively with one another in addressing the economic needs of the regions served by both.

The structure of the new economy depends heavily on the way that regional institutions—suppliers, producers, advertisers, distributors, entrepreneurs, investors, government, civic organizations, consumers—interact with one another. Especially important as a key organizational dimension of economic development is the emergence of enterprise clusters of interacting firms. Local governments and other civic institutions play a major role in determining the capacity of these economic players and systems and the productivity of their interaction.

Each jurisdiction and region also needs to confront widely varying conditions. In some, rapid growth is creating traffic congestion, environmental degradation, and rising infrastructure costs, which are in turn producing calls for growth management. In other communities, the loss of high-wage jobs and rising unemployment are creating desperate economic circumstances.

Local jurisdictions play a critical role in responding to these varying conditions and to the broader economic forces that are affecting all local economies. In a highly competitive economy, small actions matter. If your competitor is just about as good as you are, marginal actions can produce a decisive advantage—and in a period of economic transition, the opportunity is all the greater for the competitor who makes the decisive change the quickest. Local communities that are not willing to adapt will be outpaced by communities that are.

New economic roles for local leaders

Local leaders have four important roles to play in meeting these new economic challenges.

The first role is that of economic *strategist*. As strategists, local leaders need to diagnose the forces that affect the local economy, conceive a vision of what the local economy can and should become, translate that vision into practical actions, monitor those actions to ensure that they are producing the desired result, and modify the strategy appropriately if they are not.

The second economic role is to provide community *leadership*, building the consensus and support required to develop and implement strategy. Many actions critical to the local economy are partially or totally beyond the direct control of local government. Their impact depends on the effectiveness of nongovernmental institutions, including business, labor, education, nonprofit organizations, and other civic institutions working individually and in cooperation with one another. The visioning, consensus-building, and negotiating skills of local leaders in building alliances and partnerships will be crucial in getting these groups to work toward common economic goals.

The third economic role of local leaders is that of representative or *ambassador* of their jurisdiction. Many of the most important policies that affect local economies lie beyond the immediate control of the local jurisdiction altogether. These include the policies of neighboring local governments, of state government (and possibly neighboring states), of regional institutions, of the federal government, and—potentially—of foreign governments and international institutions.

The fourth economic role is *manager* of key government functions with economic impact. These include not only those functions conventionally associated with economic development such as recruitment, business financing, technical assistance, technology transfer, and marketing information, but also other local government functions that may be equally or more important, including public education and other human resource programs; physical infrastructure, such as roads, water resource systems, housing, and telecommunications networks; the channels of knowledge and technology, such as universities and research institutions; the availability of capital through a variety of private as well as public institutions; and the overall livability of the environment and community.

Providing these services effectively and efficiently is one of the most important economic responsibilities of local government.

Rethinking the basics

Economic development is the process of transforming assets into higher valued uses. Its purposes are variously viewed as producing higher living standards and quality of life; goods and services of higher quality, greater variety, and lower cost; more and/or better jobs; higher incomes; more productive enterprises; a more diverse economic base; advanced skills that will prepare workers for economic change; the opportunity to alleviate poverty and increase equity; a stronger tax base; and the capacity for sustained economic development in the future. Several powerful forces are compelling local leaders to rethink the basic assumptions underlying their approach to economic development in pursuit of these goals.

New technology is creating new industries and transforming old industries. In particular, microelectronics in combination with photonics is revolutionizing information processing and telecommunications—as well as virtually every economic activity they touch. Changing consumer tastes are increasing product specialization, and producers are searching for niche markets and differentiated products tailored to ever more specialized consumer tastes and producer needs.

The globalization of production, financial markets, marketing, and knowledge is being driven in part by technology that renders communication quick, effective, and inexpensive. Regions have become more important units of economic geography, in part because globalization renders national boundaries less significant in determining market boundaries. Thus, the greater St. Louis region today is competing with Kita Kyushu and Emilia Romagna as well as with Puget Sound and eastern Massachusetts.

Excess capacity in key industries is intensifying competition and creating pressure for personnel cutbacks and productivity improvement. This has occurred not only in such traditional manufacturing sectors as steel and automobiles, but in many service industries—including real estate, investment banking, accounting, consulting, and law. There is a continuing shift in the relative proportion of employment from manufacturing to services, although manufacturing has held its own as a proportion of gross national product. There is a widening wage gap between high-paying jobs requiring advanced knowledge and skills and low-paying jobs requiring little knowledge and skill.

Demographic change—including the aging of the population, an increasing proportion of minorities, the growing proportion of women in the labor force, and the disintegration of the family—is profoundly affecting labor and consumer markets. Although the global rate of population growth is slowing, the Third World will add 700 million new workers to the global economy during the next two decades.

In "The Changed World Economy," Peter Drucker probes some of the deeper currents of global economic restructuring. Among the developments Drucker addresses are the relative decline in the importance of primary products (raw materials such as minerals and agricultural products), the decline in manufacturing employment created by rising productivity, and the surge in global financial transactions that seem to have become detached from conventional trade.

Forces such as these—and the new economy they are creating—are compelling local governments to rethink their goals for economic development and their assumptions about how the economy works. As Drucker notes, the economy is restructuring faster than theorists can describe it or adapt their theories to explain it. But in the meantime, practitioners in both business and government must act on the new realities, whatever conventional theory may indicate.

Edward Blakely surveys the conventional theoretical underpinnings of regional and local economic development policy—including neoclassical, economic base, location, cumulative causation, and attraction theories—and concludes that none is by itself a satisfactory guide for policy. Blakely's survey provides a useful quick reference for practitioners who want to get the essence of these theories. In addition, he offers the beginnings of a simple theoretical synthesis of useful aspects of all of the theories. Blakely's proposed synthesis is based on a central theme: "Communities must use their current human, social, institutional, and physical resources to build a self-sustaining economic system."

This task is all the more important at a time when economic restructuring is creating new forms of economic organization and dynamics both within and among firms. Individual firms are stressing high performance, total quality management, continuous improvement, and related organizational changes that favor decentralization and greater responsibility and latitude for front-line workers. Meanwhile, small and medium-sized firms have been creating complex clusters and networks among themselves, often in conjunction with new alliances as suppliers of large firms.

Richard Hatch's article on flexible manufacturing networks describes one form of economic clustering that is unfamiliar to most local government officials in the United States. In Italy, Germany, Denmark, and some other countries, clusters of small and medium-sized businesses have learned to work together in "producer networks" of varying degrees of formality to design, produce, and market semi-finished and final products. They not only collectively produce parts and components to sell to large firms, but also manufacture consumer products to market directly throughout the world.

Many of the producer networks, in turn, have developed complementary "service networks" that provide the participants with shared services—such as materials testing, technology updates, market information, and financing—that they could not get as cheaply, effectively, or at all on their own. Moreover, they integrate these services in a package provided to the production network as a whole. The service networks provide what the businesses in the cluster need because the business owners themselves are members of the board of directors of the professionally operated service centers. This "bottom-up," market-driven approach is complemented by a "top-down" strategic approach reflected by the presence of government officials, academics, and industry analysts on the board as well.

This new pattern of economic organization does not suggest that Americans simply take foreign models such as flexible manufacturing networks and apply them wholesale to their own circumstances. But it does challenge traditional economic development theory and the American practice whereby government agencies that presume to know what business needs provide functionally fragmented services to individual firms. And it suggests the need to consider ways in which collaboration, alliances, and more sophisticated forms of interconnection can help American firms increase their economic potential. The most important point demonstrated by all three of these articles is that the world of economic development policy is changing quickly and dramatically, and competing local governments and regions around the world are experimenting with fundamentally different approaches.

Economic foundations

The essence of the new approach to economic development lies in understanding changing economic dynamics and ensuring that public actions promote and support a market-driven private sector in its efforts to adapt to those dynamics productively and competitively.

The private sector depends on several economic foundations that local government can affect in critical ways, including the workforce, knowledge and technology, enterprise development, financial capital, physical infrastructure, natural resources, the regulatory environment, and the quality of life.

None of these foundations is more important than the workforce. In the 1970s and early 1980s, new jobs were needed not only to replace those that had been lost when businesses failed or relocated, but also to accommodate a rapidly growing work force. However, after decades of rapid growth—during which the baby-boom generation moved into its working years and an increasing proportion of women went to work—the workforce has begun to grow more slowly. Nationwide, labor force growth fell from a peak of 2.5 percent in the 1970s to about 1.4 percent per year by the late 1980s and is projected to fall to about 1 percent in the 1990s.

In this new environment, the attention of many jurisdictions has expanded from simply creating jobs to ensuring that workers have the skills necessary to fill available jobs. The growing shortage of skilled labor is a major concern in many industries and communities, and the quality—not just the quantity—of jobs is the focus of increasing attention. Even chronically depressed regions and rural and inner-city communities are concerned about generating "good jobs" that require high skills and pay high wages.

But such jobs are not likely to be created in the absence of skilled workers to fill them, or workers who at least have the basic skills required to adapt quickly to them. Most communities now acknowledge the importance of human investment as a cornerstone of economic development policy.

Human investment covers the full range of policies that affect human knowledge and skills—from conception to retirement and beyond. Prenatal care affects the health and learning ability of infants; education begins at birth and continues throughout life. Local leaders nationwide are now aware of the importance of ensuring that students and workers have opportunities for higher education, training, and continuous education throughout their lives.

In "Developing an Internationally Competitive Workforce," William E. Nothdurft focuses on one critical dimension of human development: the link between school and the workplace. His survey of European practices uncovers techniques that might be applicable in the United States—such as apprenticeships to ensure that students learn up-to-date skills. But Nothdurft's article is equally important as a reminder of the tenacity with which our European competitors are building workforce competence. The contrast between the seriousness and impact of the European experience and the still struggling attempts by the United States to reform public schools underscores the hard reality that *relative* as well as absolute effort is crucial in determining competitive advantage. Finally, Nothdurft's findings reinforce the importance of collaboration—between the public and private sectors and between education and business—if students are to be adequately prepared for the workforce. Such collaboration must be rooted at the local level.

Technology is another key economic foundation. Walter Plosila's "Technology Development: Perspectives on the Third Wave," suggests principles for state and local technology efforts that reinforce the importance of merging the correct policy and emphasizes the important institutional connection between state policies and local consortia or networks for that purpose. Small and medium-sized businesses in particular need effective linkages with sources of knowledge and technology to make practical and continuous improvement in their products, services, and operations. The local role here is critical in two ways: (1) helping to establish local networks for firms and technology resources and (2) ensuring that state policies are designed to promote both commercial application and the appropriate institutional arrangements.

Economic development programs have tended to overlook or bypass the poor. Rather than view disadvantaged populations as potential economic resources and initiate efforts to bring them within the realm of mainstream policies, most poverty programs view disadvantages populations as problems falling outside mainstream economic development programs. David Osborne's "A Poverty Program That Works" describes a different model—one that recognizes the economic potential in disadvantaged residents and tailors market incentives and an investment philosophy to the conditions of a low-income neighborhood. Osborne characterizes the Shorebank Corporation in Chicago's South Shore neighborhood as a "holding company" that combines a bank, a real estate development corporation, and a small venture-capital firm; the Shorebank Corporation also has the capacity for housing development, remedial education, and vocational training. Because it is largely self-financing, Shorebank employs the market discipline of a firm, seeks out investments in the most promising people and assets, and supports its investments with the social infrastructure to enhance the likelihood of success.

The new economic geography

Most local jurisdictions cover no more than a slice of the economic region of which they are a part. Although the economic character of that slice of territory matters greatly, the overall and long-term economic health of each political subdivision will inevitably be affected by the economic character and fortunes of the entire region of which it is a part. Defining the economic region, or regions, on which the local economy depends and designing strategies that take into account that geographic reality is one of the keys to effective local economic strategy. The absence of such regional definition is one of the principal deficiencies in American economic development policy.

The urban region is a basic unit of economic geography, comprising common labor, commuter, advertising, communications, supplier, producer, and consumer markets. But urban regions today rarely correspond to the conventional concept of a metropolitan area made up of a central city surrounded by suburbs and sharply encompassed by a rural countryside. The "central city" is now home to less than 40 percent of the typical metropolitan population, and its historic function as the employment base has been supplanted by suburban employment nodes.

It is not unusual today for the suburban portion of a metropolitan area to have surpassed the central city in total jobs as well as population. Most metropolitan areas are composed of multiple nodes or corridors of high-density employment development—of which the traditional downtown is but one—interspersed in a sea of relatively low-density residential and commercial development that extends to exurbia and fades imperceptibly into a surrounding countryside of multiple low-density land uses—of which agriculture is but one.

In "The Suburban Growth Corridor: Defining the New Economic Geometry," George Sternlieb and James W. Hughes describe the physical infrastructure of "a suburbanized economy" that they believe has already shaped America's regional economies for the 1990s. The suburbanized economy is made up of the Interstate Highway System, including the "beltways" that have become the new main streets of the metropolitan economy; an explosion of office buildings, which are likely to be in oversupply well into the 1990s and whose location is defined largely by interstate highway patterns; a vast housing stock sprawled beyond suburbia into "ruburbia" (a blend of rural, exurban, and suburban forms of development); and the schools, water and sewer lines, and other basic infrastructure that accompany such growth. It is this economic infrastructure, already largely in place, that will define what is "local" for many regional and local economies well into the next decade and possibly the next century.

These developments highlight the increasing economic dominance of the suburbs as the place where Americans live, work, and consume. They also suggest that the oversupply of office, retail, and residential building space may dampen physical expansion in the future. For local jurisdictions that have equated economic development with real estate growth, this may be a troubling omen. For those already facing residents' concerns about the financial costs and environmental consequences of growth and congestion, a respite from development pressure may be at hand.

For distressed central cities, suburban expansion appears to have little effect but to draw investment away from the traditional central business district and inner-city neighborhoods. However, the suburban overbuilding of the eighties and the accumulated costs of serving it in the future may improve the competitive cost advantage of some central cities.

Most American metropolitan areas lack the institutional base to develop and implement regional economic strategy. In few metropolitan areas are there regionwide institutions that can take account of the full geographic sweep of regional economic dynamics. Rather than work cooperatively to develop the economy of the entire region, local jurisdictions typically compete with one another to attract business.

One consequence is that communities and neighborhoods with special needs, especially those in the central city, frequently lack the institutional support to deal with localized problems. Neal Peirce and Carol Steinbach conducted a study for the Ford Foundation that examined the role of community development corporations (CDCs) in addressing the needs of distressed communities located principally in the central cities of the Northeast and Midwest (although CDCs are also found in urban and rural areas throughout the country). "The Rise of America's Community Development Corporations" gives an upbeat assessment of the potential of CDCs for economic development in distressed communities but argues that supporting policies and investment are required for CDCs to deal realistically with the economic deprivation characteristic of the areas they serve.

CDCs have become more prominent in recent years as a holistic approach to central-city economic and social needs. Their potential has been strengthened by national intermediaries such as the Local Initiatives Support Corporation and the Enterprise Foundation. CDCs have also been supported by private financing: for example, seven private philanthropic organizations and the Prudential Insurance Company provided $62.5 million in grants and loans to establish the National Community Development Initiative.

Some regions are composed of small- to medium-sized towns forming a broader economic complex. Terry Buss and Roger Vaughan's "Revitalizing the Mahoning Valley" describes the process of economic restructuring that occurred in a multi-community region that once thrived on traditional manufacturing but had been brutally hollowed out by global economic forces.

The Mahoning Valley in northeast Ohio was part of America's industrial heartland. During the 1970s and 1980s, one after another of its steel plants closed as the industry was transformed by changing technology, shifting product demand, and foreign competition. Local economic development strategies aimed at reviving the industry or replacing it with other durable goods manufacturing failed. Buss and Vaughan analyze the reasons for the failure and describe an alternative strategy to rebuild the local entrepreneurial tradition, strengthen the economic base, create economic opportunity for the economically disadvantaged, and improve public services and the quality of life.

The organizational challenge

The new local economic responsibilities described in these articles range far beyond conventional economic development concerns. Local governments cannot effectively perform these responsibilities with conventional organizational approaches geared to the old economy and more limited economic functions. The new approaches to economic strategy require a new approach to organization. Indeed, they involve fundamental new challenges to governance.

The new institutions need to equip local officials with both a "top-down" strategic vision and a "bottom-up," market-driven, performance-oriented approach. The "top-down" approach is visionary, long-term, and comprehensive. It provides guidance, strategic direction, and organizational context. It draws on the knowledge and experience of elected officials, professional managers, analysts, synthesists, theorists, and system designers. The "bottom-up" approach is market driven. It relies on market signals—defining the needs of employers, workers, consumers, and others who respond to the market—to drive policy and determine specific actions. It places greater responsibility in the hands of government officials and service deliverers at the point of contact with target groups and individuals.

The two approaches—strategic, from the top down, and market driven, from the bottom up—are complementary, informing, challenging, and reinforcing one another. Together, they can help local government diagnose economic conditions and options, articulate a vision and set strategic direction, establish the organizational context in which the market will drive policy, assess the consequences, and make necessary adjustments.

Some of the new organizational approaches are inherent in the innovations described in the articles: service centers to meet the needs of flexible specialization networks; public-private apprenticeship programs to link school and work; networks to translate technology into marketable products; the use of market models to address problems of poverty; a strategic plan for regional economic development; community development corporations to provide a holistic approach to inner-city problems.

To take into account the numerous forces that are affecting their economies and to ensure that the wide-ranging actions they take are collectively supportive of economic development, local governments need an economic strategy. There are numerous approaches to strategic planning and its associated tasks. By asking how they can later judge the success of their strategic planning efforts, local officials can provide themselves with more disciplined guidelines for approaching this threshold organizational task. David R. Kolzow's article, "Monitoring and Evaluating Performance in the Economic Development Program," provides one set of such guidelines.

In "Organizing and Staffing Economic Development Programs," Robert R. Weaver discusses a range of conventional approaches that local governments in Texas have used to organize their economic development efforts. Most of these organizational approaches allow the local governments to undertake strategic planning, especially those that involve representatives from both the public and private sectors. But they are geared principally toward carrying out such functions as infrastructure improvement, neighborhood development, historic preservation, commercial revitalization, health and human service improvements, convention and tourism promotion, and the attraction and retention of new business.

One of the implications of Weaver's discussion is that local government managers, especially those in Texas, increasingly view economic development as organizationally centered in their immediate office, rather than in a formally designated economic development agency. The more broadly defined the scope of economic development policy, the more difficult it becomes to squeeze it into a single agency. More and more, economic development involves both the public and private sectors, for which the local government manager's office is a natural crossroads. Equally important, the local government manager's office is the intersection of numerous local government functions that are now recognized to affect economic development, as well as the central command point for coordinating intergovernmental activities—also of growing economic importance.

Another central organizational task is to assess the results of economic programs. "Evaluating Nonfinancial Business Assistance Programs," by Harry Hatry, Mark Fall, Thomas O. Singer, and E. Blaine Liner, provides some specifics on how to assess one type of program, but the methodology can be applied to other types as well.

These three articles reflect the variation and evolution of conventional organization for local economic policy. In "The Emerging Third Wave: New Economic Development Strategies in the '90s," Robert Friedman and Doug Ross argue that economic development practice is now entering a "Third Wave" that is characterized by a markedly different organizational approach. The First Wave of economic development, stretching from the 1930s to the 1970s, championed industrial recruitment. The Second Wave, beginning in the seventies and continuing into the present, shifted the focus to internal development and the provision of foundations such as trained labor, technology, and financial capital. However, many of the Second Wave programs, while headed in the right policy direction, have lacked impact because they were of insufficient scale, highly fragmented, and lacked accountability.

According to Ross and Friedman, a Third Wave of economic development practice is now underway, characterized by more effective means of organization, public technology, and management to pursue the Second Wave strategy of internal development. Early Third Wave innovations focus on approaches that are demand driven, leverage public resources, promote competition, and build in automatic feedback to improve performance. In short, the challenge to economic development in the future will be not only to develop new *policies*, but also to develop innovations in public and private *institutions* that will promote the emergence and application of effective new policies.

Conclusion

This collection of articles does not pretend to provide a comprehensive treatment of the complex field of local economic development. What it does provide is an overview of a rapidly changing field and detailed treatment of selected topics that local leaders should know about. Together, these articles should inform local leaders of key issues shaping the economic development field and alert them to the fundamentally new economic role that they will be called upon to play in the years ahead.

PART 1

Rethinking the Basics

The Changed World Economy

— Peter F. Drucker

The talk today is of the "changing world economy." I wish to argue that the world economy is not "changing"; it has *already changed*—in its foundations and in its structure—and in all probability the change is irreversible.

Within the last decade or so, three fundamental changes have occurred in the very fabric of the world economy:

The primary-products economy has come "uncoupled" from the industrial economy.

In the industrial economy itself, production has come "uncoupled" from employment.

Capital movements rather than trade (in both goods and services) have become the driving force of the world economy. The two have not quite come uncoupled, but the link has become loose, and worse, unpredictable.

These changes are permanent rather than cyclical. We may never understand what caused them—the causes of economic change are rarely simple. It may be a long time before economic theorists accept that there have been fundamental changes, and longer still before they adapt their theories to account for them. Above all, they will surely be most reluctant to accept that is the world economy in control, rather than the macroeconomics of the nation-state on which most economic theory still exclusively focuses. Yet this is the clear lesson of the success stories of the last 20 years—of Japan and South Korea; of West Germany (actually a more impressive though far less flamboyant example than Japan); and of the one great success within the United States, the turnaround and rapid rise of an industrial New England, which only 20 years ago was widely considered moribund.

Practitioners, whether in government or in business, cannot wait until there is a new theory. They have to act. And their actions will be more likely to succeed the more they are based on the new realities of a changed world economy.

First, consider the primary-products economy. The collapse of non-oil commodity prices began in 1977 and has continued, interrupted only once (right after the 1979 petroleum panic), by a speculative burst that lasted less than six months; it was followed by the fastest drop in commodity prices ever registered. By early 1986 raw material prices were at their lowest levels in recorded history in relation to the prices of manufactured good and services—in general as low as at the depths of the Great Depression, and in some cases (e.g., lead and copper) lower than their 1932 levels.[1] . . .

Remarkably, the raw materials economy seems to have had almost no impact on the world industrial economy. If there was one thing considered "proven" beyond doubt in business cycle theory, it is that a sharp and prolonged drop in raw material prices inevitably, and within 18 to 30 months, brings on a worldwide depression in the industrial economy.[2] While the industrial economy of the world today is not "normal" by any definition of the term, it is surely not in a depression. Indeed, industrial production in the developed non-communist countries has continued to grow steadily, albeit at a somewhat slower rate in Western Europe.

Of course, a depression in the industrial economy may only have been postponed and may still be triggered by a banking crisis caused by massive defaults on the part of commodity-producing debtors, whether in the Third World or in Iowa. But for almost ten years the industrial world has run along as though there were no raw materials crisis at all. The only explanation is that for the developed countries—excepting only the Soviet Union—the primary-products sector has become marginal where before it had always been central. . . .

What accounts for this change?

Demand for food has actually grown. . . . But the supply has grown much faster; it not only has kept pace with population growth, it has steadily outrun it. One cause of this, paradoxically, is surely the fear of worldwide food shortages, if not world famine, which resulted in tremendous efforts to increase food output. The United States led the parade with a farm policy of subsidizing increased food production. The European Economic Community followed suit, and even more successfully. The greatest increases, both in absolute and in relative terms, however, have been in developing countries: in India, in post-Mao China and in the rice-growing countries of Southeast Asia.

And there is also the tremendous cut in waste. In the 1950s, up to 80 percent of grain harvest of India fed rats and insects rather than human beings. Today in most parts of India the wastage is down to 20 percent. This is largely the result of unspectacular but effective "infrastructure innovations" such as small concrete storage bins, insecticides and three-wheeled motorized carts that take the harvest straight to a processing plant instead of letting it sit in the open for weeks.

It is not fanciful to expect that the true "revolution" on the farm is still ahead. Vast tracts of land that hitherto were practically barren are being made fertile, either through new methods of cultivation or through adding trace minerals to the soil. The sour clays of the Brazilian highlands or the aluminum-contaminated soils of neighboring Peru, for example, which never produced anything before, now produce substantial quantities of high-quality rice. Even greater advances have been registered in biotechnology, both in preventing diseases of plants and animals and in increasing yields.

In other words, just as the population growth of the world is slowing down quite dramatically in many regions, food production is likely to increase sharply. . . .

For practically all non-farm commodities, whether forest products, minerals or metals, world demand is shrinking. Indeed, the amount of raw material needed for a given unit of economic output has been dropping for the entire century, except in wartime. A recent study by the International Monetary Fund calculates the decline as one and one-quarter percent a year (compounded) since 1900.[3] This would mean that the amount of industrial raw materials needed for one unit of industrial production is now no more than two-fifths of what it was in 1900. And the decline is accelerating. The Japanese experience is particularly striking. In 1984, for every unit of industrial production, Japan consumed only 60 percent of the raw materials consumed for the same volume of industrial production in 1973, 11 years earlier.

Why this decline in demand? It is not that industrial production is fading in importance as the service sector grows—a common myth for which there is not the slightest evidence. What is happening is much more significant. Industrial production is steadily switching away from heavily material-intensive products and processes. One of the reasons for this is the new high-technology industries. The raw materials in a semiconductor microchip account for one to three percent of total production cost; in an automobile their share is 40 percent, and in pots and pans 60 percent. But also in older industries the same scaling down of raw material needs goes on, and with respect to old products as well as new ones. Fifty to 100 pounds of fiberglass cable transmit as many telephone messages as does one ton of copper wire.

This steady drop in the raw material intensity of manufacturing processes and manufacturing products extends to energy as well, and especially to petroleum. To produce 100 pounds of fiberglass cable requires no more than five percent of the energy needed to produce one ton of copper wire. Similarly, plastics, which are increasingly replacing steel in automobile bodies, represent a raw material cost, including energy, of less than half that of steel.

Thus it is quite unlikely that raw material prices will ever rise substantially as compared to the prices of manufactured goods (or high-knowledge services such as information, education or health care) except in the event of a major prolonged war.

One implication of this sharp shift in the terms of trade of primary products concerns the developed countries, both major raw material exporters like the United States and major raw material importing countries such as Japan. For two centuries the United States has made maintenance of open markets for its farm products and raw materials central to its international trade policy. This is what it has always meant by an "open world economy" and by "free trade."

Does this still make sense, or does the United States instead have to accept that foreign markets for its foodstuffs and raw materials are in a long-term and irreversible decline? Conversely, does it still make sense for Japan to base its international economic policy on the need to earn enough foreign exchange to pay for imports of raw materials and foodstuffs? Since Japan opened to the outside world 120 years ago, preoccupation—amounting almost to a national obsession—with its dependence on raw material and food imports has been the driving force of Japan's policy, and not in economics alone. Now Japan might well start out with the assumption—a far more realistic one in today's world—that foodstuffs and raw materials are in permanent oversupply.

Take to their logical conclusion, these developments might mean that some variant of the traditional Japanese policy—highly mercantilist with a strong de-emphasis of domestic consumption in favor of an equally strong emphasis on capital formulation, and protection of infant industries—might suit the United States better than its own tradition. The Japanese might be better served by some variant of America's traditional policies, especially a shifting from favoring savings and capital formation to favoring consumption. Is such a radical break with more than a century of political convictions and commitments likely? From now on the fundamentals of economic policy are certain to come under increasing criticism in these two countries—and in all other developed countries as well.

These fundamentals will, moreover, come under the increasingly intense scrutiny of major Third World nations. For if primary products are becoming of marginal importance to the economies of the developed world, traditional development theories and policies are losing their foundations.[4] They are based on the assumption— historically a perfectly valid one—that developing countries pay for imports of capital goods by exporting primary materials—farm and forest products, minerals, metals. All development theories, however much they differ otherwise, further assume that raw material purchases by the industrially developed countries must rise at least as fast as industrial production in these countries. This in turn implies that, over any extended period of time, any raw material producer becomes a better credit risk and shows a more favorable balance of trade. These premises have become highly doubtful. On what foundation, then, can economic development be based, especially in countries that do not have a large enough population to develop an industrial economy based on the home market? As we shall presently see, these countries can no longer base their economic development on low labor costs.

The second major change in the world economy is the uncoupling of manufacturing production from manufacturing employment. Increased manufacturing production in developed countries has actually come to mean *decreasing* blue-collar employment. As a consequence, labor costs are becoming less and less important as a "comparative cost" and as a factor in competition.

There is a great deal of talk these days about the "de-industrialization" of America. In fact, manufacturing production has risen steadily in absolute volume and has remained unchanged as a percentage of the total economy. Since the end of the Korean War, that is, for more than 30 years, it has held steady at 23–24 percent of America's total GNP. It has similarly remained at its traditional level in all of the other major industrial countries.

It is not even true that American industry is doing poorly as an exporter. To be sure, the United States is importing from both Japan and Germany many more manufactured goods than ever before. But it is also exporting more, despite the heavy disadvantages of an expensive dollar, increasing labor costs and the near-collapse of a major industrial market, Latin America. In 1984—the year the dollar soared—exports of American manufactured goods rose by 8.3 percent; and they went up again in 1985. The share of U.S.-manufactured exports in world exports was 17 percent in 1978. By 1985 it had risen to 20 percent—while West Germany accounted for 18 percent and Japan 16. The three countries together thus account for more than half of the total.

Thus it is not the American economy that is being "de-industrialized." It is the American labor force.

Between 1973 and 1985, manufacturing production (measured in constant dollars) in the United States rose by almost 40 percent. Yet manufacturing employment during that period went down steadily. There are now five million fewer people employed in blue-collar work in American manufacturing industry than there were in 1975.

Yet from 1973 to 1985 total employment in the United States

grew faster than at any time in the peacetime history of any country—from 82 to 110 million—that is, by a full one-third. The entire growth, however, was in non-manufacturing, and especially in non–blue-collar jobs. . . .

This trend is the same in all developed countries, and is, indeed, even more pronounced in Japan. It is therefore highly probable that in 25 years developed countries such as the United States and Japan will employ no larger a proportion of the labor force in manufacturing than developed countries now employ in farming—at most, ten percent. Today the United States employs around 18 million people in blue-collar jobs in manufacturing industries. By 2010, the number is likely to be no more than 12 million. In some major industries the drop will be even sharper. It is quite unrealistic, for instance, to expect that the American automobile industry will employ more than one-third of its present blue-collar force 25 years hence, even though production might be 50 percent higher.

If a company, an industry or a country does not in the next quarter century sharply increase manufacturing production and at the same time sharply reduce the blue-collar work force, it cannot hope to remain competitive—or even to remain "developed." It would decline fairly fast. Britain has been in industrial decline for the last 25 years, largely because the number of blue-collar workers per unit of manufacturing production went down far more slowly than in all other non-communist developed countries. Even so, Britain has the highest unemployment rate among non-communist developed countries—more than 13 percent.

The British example indicates a new and critical economic equation: a country, an industry, or a company that puts the preservation of blue-collar manufacturing jobs ahead of international competitiveness (which implies a steady shrinkage of such jobs) will soon have neither production nor jobs. The attempt to preserve such blue-collar jobs is actually a prescription for unemployment.

So far, this concept has achieved broad national acceptance only in Japan.[5] Indeed, Japanese planners, whether in government or private business, start out with the assumption of a doubling of production within 15 or 20 years based on a cut in blue-collar employment of 25 to 40 percent. A good many large American companies such as IBM, General Electric and the big automobile companies have similar forecasts. Implicit in this is the conclusion that a country will have less overall unemployment the faster it shrinks blue-collar employment in manufacturing.

This is not a conclusion that American politicians, labor leaders or indeed the general public can easily understand or accept. What confuses the issue even more is that the United States is experiencing several separate and different shifts in the manufacturing economy. One is the acceleration of the substitution of knowledge and capital for manual labor. Where we spoke of mechanization a few decades ago, we now speak of "robotization" or "automation." This is actually more a change in terminology than a change in reality. When Henry Ford introduced the assembly line in 1909, he cut the number of man-hours required to produce a motor car by some 80 percent in two or three years—far more than anyone expects to result from even the most complete robotization. But there is no doubt that we are facing a new, sharp acceleration in the replacement of manual workers by machines—that is, by the products of knowledge.

A second development—and in the long run this may be even more important—is the shift from industries that were primarily labor-intensive to industries that, from the beginning, are knowledge-intensive. The manufacturing costs of the semiconductor microchip are about 70 percent knowledge—that is, research, development and testing—and no more than 12 percent labor. Similarly with prescription drugs, labor represents no more than 15 percent, with knowledge representing almost 50 percent. By contrast, in the most fully robotized automobile plant, labor would still account for 20 or 25 percent of the costs.

Another perplexing development in manufacturing is the reversal of the dynamics of size. Since the early years of this century, the trend in all developed countries has been toward ever larger manufacturing plants. The economies of scale greatly favored them. Perhaps equally important, what one might call the "economies of management" favored them. Until recently, modern management techniques seemed applicable only to fairly large units.

This has been reversed with a vengeance over the last 15 to 20 years. The entire shrinkage in manufacturing jobs in the United States has occurred in large companies, beginning with the giants in steel and automobiles. Small and especially medium-sized manufacturers have either held their own or actually added employees. In respect to market standing, exports and profitability too, smaller and middle-sized businesses have done remarkably better than big ones. The reversal of the dynamics of size is occurring in the other developed countries as well, even in Japan where bigger was always better and biggest meant best. . . .

In part, especially in the United States, this is a result of a resurgence of entrepreneurship.[6] But perhaps equally important, we have learned in the last 30 years how to manage the small and medium-sized enterprise to the point where the advantages of smaller size, e.g., ease of communications and nearness to market and customer, increasingly outweigh what had been forbidding management limitations. Thus in the United States, but increasingly in the other leading manufacturing nations such as Japan and West Germany as well, the dynamism in the economy has shifted from the very big companies that dominated the world's industrial economy for 30 years after World War II to companies that, while much smaller, are professionally managed and largely publicly financed.

Two distinct kinds of "manufacturing industry" are emerging. One is material-based, represented by the industries that provided economic growth in the first three-quarters of this century. The other is information- and knowledge-based: pharmaceuticals, telecommunications, analytical instruments and information processing such as computers. It is largely the information-based manufacturing industries that are growing.

These two groups differ not only in their economic characteristics but especially in their position in the international economy. The products of material-based industries have to be exported or imported as "products." They appear in the balance of trade. The products of information-based industries can be exported or imported both as "products" and as "services," which may not appear accurately in the overall trade balance.

An old example is the printed book. For one major scientific publishing company, "foreign earnings" account for two-thirds of total revenues. Yet the company exports few, if any, actual books—books are heavy. It sells "rights," and the "product" is produced abroad. Similarly, the most profitable computer "export sales" may actually show up in trade statistics as an "import." This is the fee some of the world's leading banks, multinationals and Japanese trading companies get for processing in their home office data arriving electronically from their branches and customers around the world.

In all developed countries, "knowledge" workers have already become the center of gravity of the labor force. Even in manufacturing they will outnumber blue-collar workers within ten years. Exporting knowledge so that it produces license income, service fees and royalties may actually create substantially more jobs than exporting goods.

This in turn requires—as official Washington seems to have realized—far greater emphasis in trade policy on "invisible trade" and on abolishing the barriers to the trade in services. Traditionally, economists have treated invisible trade as a stepchild, if they noted it at all. Increasingly, it will become central. Within 20 years major developed countries may find that their income from invisible trade is larger than their income from exports.

Another implication of the "uncoupling" of manufacturing production from manufacturing employment is, however, that the choice between an industrial policy that favors industrial *production* and one that favors industrial *employment* is going to be a singularly contentious political issue for the rest of this century. Historically these have always been considered two sides of the same coin. From now on these two will increasingly pull in different directions; they are indeed already becoming alternatives, if not incompatible.

Benign neglect—the policy of the Reagan Administration these last few years—may be the best policy one can hope for, and the only one with a chance of success. It is probably not an accident that the United States has, after Japan, by far the lowest unemployment rate of any industrially developed country. Still, there is surely need also for systematic efforts to retrain and to place redundant blue-collar workers—something no one as yet knows how to do success-fully.

Finally, low labor costs are likely to become less of an advantage in international trade simply because in the developed countries they are going to account for less of total costs. Moreover, the total costs of automated processes are lower than even those of traditional plants with low labor costs; this is mainly because automation eliminates the hidden but high costs of "not working," such as the expense of poor quality and rejects, and the costs of shutting down the machinery to change from one model of a product to another. Consider two automated American producers of televisions, Motorola and RCA. Both were almost driven out of the market by imports from countries with much lower labor costs. Both subsequently automated, with the result that these American-made products now successfully compete with foreign imports. Similarly, some highly automated textile mills in the Carolinas can underbid imports from countries with very low labor costs such as Thailand. On the other hand, although some American semiconductor companies have lower labor costs because they do the labor-intensive work off-shore, e.g., in West Africa, they are still the high-cost producers and easily underbid by the heavily automated Japanese.

The cost of capital will thus become increasingly important in international competition. And this is where, in the last ten years, the United States has become the highest-cost country—and Japan the lowest. A reversal of the U.S. policy of high interest rates and costly equity capital should thus be a priority for American decision-makers. This demands that reduction of the government deficit, rather than high interest rates, becomes the first defense against inflation.

For developed countries, especially the United States, the steady downgrading of labor costs as a major competitive factor could be a positive development. For the Third World, especially rapidly industrializing countries such as Brazil, South Korea or Mexico, it is, however, bad news.

In the rapid industrialization of the nineteenth century, one country, Japan, developed by exporting raw materials, mainly silk and tea, at steadily rising prices. Another, Germany, developed by leapfrogging into the "high-tech" industries of its time, mainly electricity, chemicals and optics. A third, the United States, did both. Both routes are blocked for today's rapidly industrializing countries—the first because of the deterioration of the terms of trade for primary products, the second because it requires an infrastructure of knowledge and education far beyond the reach of a poor country (although South Korea is reaching for it). Competition based on lower labor costs seems to be the only alternative; is this also going to be blocked?

The third major change that has occurred in the world economy is the emergence of the "symbol" economy—capital movements, exchange rates and credit flows—as the flywheel of the world economy, in place of the "real" economy—the flow of goods and services. The two economies seem to be operating increasingly independently. This is both the most visible and the least understood of the changes.

World trade in goods is larger, much larger, than it has ever been before. And so is the "invisible trade," the trade in services. Together, the two amount to around $2.5 trillion to $3 trillion a year. But the London Eurodollar market, in which the world's financial institutions borrow from and lend to each other, turns over $300 billion each working day, or $75 trillion a year, a volume at least 25 times that of world trade.[7]

In addition, there are the foreign exchange transactions in the world's main money centers, in which one currency is traded against another. These run around $150 billion a day, or about $35 trillion a year—12 times the worldwide trade in goods and services.

Of course, many of these Eurodollars, yen and Swiss francs are just being moved from one pocket to another and may be counted more than once. A massive discrepancy still exists, and there is only one conclusion: capital movements unconnected to trade—and indeed largely independent of it—greatly exceed trade finance.

There is no one explanation for this explosion of international— or more accurately, transnational—money flows. The shift from fixed to floating exchange rates in 1971 may have given an initial impetus (though, ironically, it was meant to do the exact opposite) by inviting currency speculation. The surge in liquid funds flowing to petroleum producers after the two oil shocks of 1973 and 1979 was surely a major factor.

But there can be little doubt that the U.S. government deficit also plays a big role. The American budget has become a financial "black hole," sucking in liquid funds from all over the world, making the United States the world's major debtor country.[8] Indeed, it can be argued that it is the budget deficit that underlies the American trade and payments deficit. A trade and payments deficit is, in effect, a loan from the seller of goods and services to the buyer, that is, to the United States. Without it Washington could not finance its budget deficit, at least not without the risk of explosive inflation.

The way major countries have learned to use the international economy to avoid tackling disagreeable domestic problems is unprecedented: the United States has used high interest rates to attract foreign capital and avoid confronting its domestic deficit; the Japanese have pushed exports to maintain employment despite a sluggish domestic economy. This politicization of the international economy is surely also a factor in the extreme volatility and instability of capital flows and exchange rates.

Whichever of these causes is judged the most important, together they have produced a basic change: in the world economy of today, the "real" economy of goods and services and the "symbol" economy of money, credit and capital are no longer bound tightly to each other; they are, indeed, moving further and further apart.

Traditional international economic theory is still neoclassical, holding that trade in goods and services determines international capital flows and foreign exchange rates. Capital flows and foreign exchange rates since the first half of the 1970s have, however, moved quite independently of foreign trade, and indeed (e.g., in the rise of the dollar in 1984–85) have run counter to it.

But the world economy also does not fit the Keynesian model in which the "symbol" economy determines the "real" economy. The relationship between the turbulences in the world economy and the various domestic economies has become quite obscure. Despite its unprecedented trade deficit, the United States has had no deflation and has barely been able to keep inflation in check; it also has the lowest unemployment rate of any major industrial country except Japan, lower than that of West Germany, whose exports of manufactured goods and trade surpluses have been growing as fast as those of Japan. Conversely, despite the exponential growth of Japanese exports and an unprecedented Japanese trade surplus, the Japanese domestic economy is not booming but has remained remarkably sluggish and is not generating any new jobs.

Economists assume that the "real" economy and the "symbol" economy will come together again. They do disagree, however— and quite sharply—as to whether they will do so in a "soft landing" or in a head-on collision.

The "soft-landing" scenario—the Reagan Administration was committed to it, as are the governments of most of the other developed countries—expects the U.S. government deficit and the U.S. trade deficit to go down together until both attain surplus, or at least balance, sometime in the early 1990s. Presumably both capital flows and exchange rates will then stabilize, with production and employment high and inflation low in major developed countries.

In sharp contrast to this are the "hard-landing" scenarios.[9] With every deficit year the indebtedness of the U.S. government goes up, and with it the interest charges on the U.S. budget, which in turn raises the deficit even further. Sooner or later, the argument goes, foreign confidence in America and the American dollar will be undermined—some observers consider this practically imminent. Foreigners would stop lending money to the United States and, indeed, try to convert their dollars into other currencies. The resulting "flight from the dollar" would bring the dollar's exchange rates crashing down, and also create an extreme credit crunch, if not a "liquidity crisis" in the United States. The only question is whether the result for the United States would be a deflationary depression, a renewed outbreak of severe inflation or, the most dreaded affliction, "stagflation"—a deflationary, stagnant economy combined with an inflationary currency.

There is, however, a totally different "hard-landing" scenario, one in which Japan, not the United States, faces an economic crisis. For the first time in peacetime history the major debtor, the United States, owes its foreign debt in its own currency. To get out of this debt it does not need to repudiate it, declare a moratorium, or negotiate a "roll-over." All it has to do is devalue its currency and the foreign creditor has effectively been expropriated.

For "foreign creditor," read Japan. The Japanese by now hold about half of the dollars the United States owes to foreigners. In addition, practically all of their other claims on the outside world are in dollars, largely because the Japanese have resisted all attempts to make the yen an international trading currency lest the government lose control over it. Altogether, Japanese banks now hold more international assets than do the banks of any other country, including the United States. And practically all these assets are in U.S. dollars—$640 billion of them. A devaluation of the U.S. dollar thus would fall most heavily on the Japanese.

The repercussions for Japan extend deep into its trade and domestic economy. By far the largest part of Japan's exports goes to the United States. If there is a "hard landing," the United States might well turn protectionist almost overnight; it is unlikely that Americans would let in large volumes of imported goods were the unemployment rate to soar. But this would immediately cause severe unemployment in Tokyo and Nagoya and Hiroshima, and might indeed set off a true depression in Japan.

There is still another "hard-landing" scenario. In this version neither the United States, nor Japan, nor the industrial economies altogether, experience the "hard landing"; it would hit the already depressed producers of primary products.

Practically all primary materials are traded in dollars, and their prices might not go up at all should the dollar be devalued (they actually went down when the dollar plunged by 30 percent between summer 1985 and February 1986). Thus Japan may be practically unaffected by a dollar devaluation; Japan needs dollar balances only to pay for primary-product imports, as it buys little else on the outside and has no foreign debt. The United States, too, may not suffer, and may even benefit as its industrial exports become more competitive. But while the primary producers sell mainly in dollars, they have to pay in other developed nations' currencies for a large part of their industrial imports. The United States, after all, although the world's leading exporter of industrial goods, still accounts for only one-fifth of the total. And the dollar prices of the industrial goods furnished by others—the Germans, the Japanese, the French, the British, and so on—are likely to go up. This might bring about a further drop in the terms of trade for the already depressed primary producers. Some estimates of the possible deterioration go as high as ten percent, which would entail considerable hardship not only for metal mines in South America and Zimbabwe, but also for farmers in Canada, Kansas and Brazil.

One more possible scenario involves no "landings," either "soft" or "hard." What if the economists were wrong and both the American budget deficit and American trade deficit continue, albeit at lower levels than in recent years? This would happen if the outside worl's willingness to put its money into the United States were based on other than purely economic considerations—on their own internal domestic politics, for example, or simply on the desire to escape risks at home that appear to be far worse than a U.S. devaluation.

This is the only scenario that is so far supported by hard facts rather than by theory. Indeed, it is already playing.

The U.S. government talked the dollar down by almost one-third (from a rate of 250 yen to 180 yen to the dollar) between summer of 1985 and February 1986—one of the most massive devaluations ever of a major currency, though called a "readjustment." America's creditors unanimously supported this devaluation and indeed demanded it. More amazing still, they responded by increasing their loans to the United States, and substantially so. International bankers seem to agree that the United States is more creditworthy the more the lender stands to lose by lending to it!

A major reason for this Alice-in-Wonderland attitude is that the biggest U.S. creditors, the Japanese, clearly prefer even very heavy losses on their dollar holdings to domestic unemployment. And without exports to the United States, Japan might have unemployment close to that of Western Europe, nine to eleven percent, and concentrated in the most politically sensitive smokestack industries in which Japan is becoming increasingly vulnerable to competition from newcomers such as South Korea.

Similarly, economic conditions alone will not induce Hong Kong Chinese to withdraw the money they have transferred to American banks in anticipation of Hong Kong's reversion to Chinese sovereignty in 1997. These deposits amount to billions. The even larger amounts—at least several hundred billion—of "flight capital" from Latin America that have found refuge in the U.S. dollar will also not be lured away by purely economic incentives such as higher interest rates.

The sum needed from the outside to maintain both a huge U.S. budget deficit and a huge U.S. trade deficit would be far too big to make this the most probable scenario. But if political factors are in control, the "symbol" economy is indeed truly "uncoupled" from the "real" economy, at least in the international sphere. Whichever scenario proves right, none promises a return to any kind of "normalcy."

From now on exchange rates between major currencies will have to be treated in economic theory and business policy alike as a "comparative-advantage" factor, and a major one.

Economic theory teaches that the comparative-advantage factors of the "real" economy—comparative labor costs and labor productivity, raw material costs, energy costs, transportation costs and the like—determine exchange rates. Practically all businesses base their policies on this notion. Increasingly, however, it is exchange rates that decide how labor costs in country A compare to labor costs in country B. Exchange rates are thus a major "comparative cost" and one totally beyond business control. Any firm exposed to the international economy has to realize that it is in two businesses at the same time. It is both a maker of goods (or a supplier of services) and a "financial" business. It cannot disregard either.

Specifically, the business that sells abroad—whether as an exporter or through a subsidiary—will have to protect itself against three foreign exchange exposures: proceeds from sales, working capital devoted to manufacturing for overseas markets, and investments abroad. This will have to be done whether the business expects the value of its own currency to go up or down. Businesses that buy abroad will have to do likewise. Indeed, even purely domestic businesses that face foreign competition in their home market will have to learn to hedge against the currency in which their main competitors produce. If American businesses had been run this way during the years of the overvalued dollar, from 1982 through 1985, most of the losses in market standing abroad and in foreign earnings might have been prevented. They were management failures, not acts of God. Surely stockholders, but also the public in general, have every right to expect management to do better the next time around.

In respect to government policy there is one conclusion: don't be "clever." It is tempting to exploit the ambiguity, instability and uncertainty of the world economy to gain short-term advantages and to duck unpopular political decisions. But it does not work. Indeed, disaster is a more likely outcome than success, as all three of the attempts made so far amply indicate.

In the first attempt, the Carter Administration pushed down the U.S. dollar to artificial lows to stimulate the American economy through the promotion of exports. American exports did indeed go up—spectacularly so. But far from stimulating the domestic economy, this depressed it, resulting in simultaneous record unemployment and accelerated inflation—the worst of all possible outcomes.

President Reagan a few years later pushed up interest rates to stop inflation, and also pushed up the dollar. This did indeed stop inflation. It also triggered massive inflows of capital. But it so overvalued the dollar as to create a surge of foreign imports. As a result, the Reagan policy exposed the most vulnerable of the smokestack industries, such as steel and automobiles, to competition they could not possibly meet. It deprived them of the earnings they needed to modernize themselves. Also, the policy seriously damaged, perhaps irreversibly, the competitive position of American farm products in the world markets, and at the worst possible time. Worse still, his "cleverness" defeated Mr. Reagan's major purpose: the reduction of the U.S. government deficit. Because of the losses to foreign competition, domestic industry did not grow enough to produce higher tax revenues. Yet the easy and almost unlimited availability of foreign money enabled Congress (and the Administration) to postpone again and again action to cut the deficit.

In the third case the Japanese, too, may have been too clever in their attempt to exploit the disjunction between the international "symbol" and "real" economies. Exploiting an undervalued yen, the Japanese have been pushing exports—a policy quite reminiscent of America under the Carter Administration. But the Japanese policy similarly has failed to stimulate the domestic economy; it has been barely growing these last few years despite the export boom. As a result, the Japanese have become dangerously overdependent on one customer, the United States. This has forced them to invest huge sums in American dollars, even though every thoughtful Japanese (including, of course, individuals in the Japanese government and the Japanese central bank) has known all along that these investments would end up being severely devalued.

Surely these three lessons should have taught us that government economic policies will succeed to the extent to which they try to harmonize the needs of the two economies, rather than to the extent to which they try to exploit the disharmony between them. Or to repeat very old wisdom, "in finance don't be clever; be simple and conscientious." I am afraid this is advice that governments are not likely to heed soon.

It is much too early to guess what the world economy of tomorrow will be like. Will major countries, for instance, succumb to traditional fears and retreat into protectionism? Or will they see a changed world economy as an opportunity?

Some parts of the main agenda, however, are fairly clear by now. Rapidly industrializing countries like Mexico or Brazil will need to formulate new development concepts and policies. They can no longer hope to finance their development by raw material exports, e.g., Mexican oil. It is also becoming unrealistic for them to believe that their low labor costs will enable them to export large quantities of finished goods to developed countries—something the Brazilians, for instance, still expect. They would do much better to go into "production sharing," that is, to use their labor advantage to become subcontractors to developed-country manufacturers for highly labor-intensive work that cannot be automated—some assembly operations, for instance, or parts and components needed only in relatively small quantities. Developed countries no longer have the labor to do such work, which even with the most thorough automation will still account for 15 to 20 percent of manufacturing work.

Such production sharing is, of course, how Singapore, Hong Kong and Taiwan bootstrapped their development. Yet in Latin America production sharing is still politically unacceptable and, indeed, anathema. Mexico, for instance, has been deeply committed since its beginnings as a modern nation in the early years of this century to make its economy less dependent on, and less integrated with, that of its big neighbor to the north. That this policy has been a total failure for 80 years has only strengthened its emotional and political appeal.

Even if production sharing is implemented to the fullest, it would not by itself provide enough income to fuel development, especially of countries so much larger than the Chinese "city-states." We thus need a new model and new policies.

Can we learn something from India? Everyone knows of India's problems—and they are legion. Few people seem to realize, however, that since independence India has done a better development job than almost any other Third World country: it has enjoyed the fastest increase in farm production and farm yields; a growth rate in manufacturing production equal to that of Brazil, and perhaps even of South Korea (India now has a bigger industrial economy than any but a handful of developed countries); the emergence of a large and highly entrepreneurial middle class; and, arguably, the greatest achievement in providing schooling and health care in the villages. Yet the Indians followed none of the established models. They did not, like Stalin, Mao and so many leaders of newly independent African nations, despoil the peasants to produce capital for industrial development. They did not export raw materials. And they did not export the products of cheap labor. Instead, since Nehru's death in 1964, India has followed a policy of strengthening agriculture and encouraging consumer goods production. India and its achievement are bound to get far more attention in the future.

The developed countries, too, need to think through their policies in respect to the Third World—and especially in respect to the "stars" of the Third World, the rapidly industrializing countries.

There are some beginnings: the debt proposals put forward by [former] Treasury Secretary James A. Baker, or the new lending criteria announced by the World Bank for loans to Third World countries, which will be made conditional on a country's overall development policies rather than on the soundness of individual projects. But these proposals are aimed more at correcting past mistakes than at developing new policies.

The other major agenda item is—inevitably—the international monetary system. Since the Bretton Woods Conference in 1944, the world monetary system has been based on the U.S. dollar as the reserve currency. This clearly does not work any more. The reserve-currency country must be willing to subordinate its domestic policies to the needs of the international economy, e.g., risk domestic unemployment to keep currency rates stable. And when it came to the crunch, the United States refused to do so—as Keynes, by the way, predicted 40 years ago.

The stability supposedly supplied by the reserve currency could be established today only if the major trading countries—at a minimum the United States, West Germany and Japan—agreed to coordinate their economic, fiscal and monetary policies, if not to subordinate them to joint (and this would mean supranational) decision-making. Is this a development even conceivable, except perhaps in the event of worldwide financial collapse? The European experience with the far more modest European Currency Unit is not encouraging; so far, no European government has been willing to yield an inch for the sake of the ECU. But what else can be done? Have we come to the end of the 300-year-old attempt to regulate and stabilize money on which, after all, both the modern nation-state and the international system are largely based?

We are left with one conclusion: economic dynamics have decisively shifted from the national economy to the world economy.

Prevailing economic theory—whether Keynesian, monetarist or supply-side—considers the national economy, especially that of the large developed countries, to be autonomous and the unit of both economic analysis and economic policy. The international economy may be a restraint and a limitation, but it is not central, let alone determining. This "macroeconomic axiom" of the modern economist has become increasingly shaky. The two major subscribers to this axiom, Britain and the United States, have done least well economically in the last 30 years, and have also had the most economic instability.

West Germany and Japan never accepted the "macroeconomic axiom." Their universities teach it, of course, but their policymakers, both in government and in business, reject it. Instead, both countries all along have based their economic policies on the world economy, have systematically tried to anticipate its trends and exploit its changes as opportunities. Above all, both make the country's competitive position in the world economy the first priority in their policies—economic, fiscal, monetary, even social—to which domestic considerations are normally subordinated. And these two countries have done far better—economically and socially—than Britain and the United States these last 30 years. In fact, their focus on the world economy and the priority they gave it may be the real "secret" of their success.

Similarly the "secret" of successful businesses in the developed world—the Japanese, the German carmakers like Mercedes and BMW, Asea and Erickson in Sweden, IBM and Citibank in the United States, but equally of a host of medium-sized specialists in manufacturing and in all kinds of services—has been that they base their plans and their policies on exploiting the world economy's changes as opportunities.

From now on any country—but also any business, especially a large one—that wants to prosper will have to accept that it is the world economy that leads and that domestic economic policies will succeed only if they strengthen, or at least do not impair, the country's international competitive position. This may be the most important—it surely is the most striking—feature of the changed world economy.

1. When the price of petroleum dropped to $15 a barrel in February 1986, it was actually below its 1933 price (adjusted for the change in the purchasing power of the dollar). It was still, however, substantially higher than its all-time low in 1972–1975, which in 1986 dollars amounted to $7–$8 a barrel.

2. The business cycle theory was developed just before World War I by the Russian mathematical economist Nikolai Kondratieff, who made comprehensive studies of raw material price cycles and their impacts all the way back to 1797.

3. David Sapsford, *Real Primary Commodity Prices: An Analysis of Long-Run Movements*, International Monetary Fund memorandum, May 17, 1985 (unpublished).

4. This was asserted as early as 1950 by the South American economist Raul Prebisch in *The Economic Development of Latin America and Its Principal Problems* (United Nations Economic Commission for Latin America). But then no one, including myself, believed him.

5. The Japanese government, for example, sponsors a finance company that makes long-term, low-interest loans to small manufacturers to enable them to automate rapidly.

6. On this see my book *Innovation and Entrepreneurship: Practice and Principles* (New York: Harper and Row, 1985).

7. A Eurodollar is a U.S dollar held outside the United States.

8. This is cogently argued by Stephen Marris, for almost thirty years economic adviser to the Organization for Economic Cooperation and Development, in his *Deficits and the Dollar: The World Economy at Risk* (Washington, D.C.: Washington Institute of International Economics, 1985).

9. Stephen Marris's *Deficits and the Dollar* gives the clearest and most persuasive presentation of the hard-landing scenarios.

The Meaning of
Local
Economic
Development

Edward J. Blakely

There is increasing recognition among both national and local poli-cymakers that, whatever national economic strategies are pursued to stimulate the economy, no community large or small can depend upon these measures alone. Moreover, in too many instances, the combination of national economic interest and the motivations of multinational firms do not coincide with the needs or interest of local communities, workers, or disadvantaged segments of the commu-nity. In market-driven economies, communities are marketplaces too. As a result, communities must put themselves in a position to market their resources intelligently and gain *competitive advantages* to create new firms and maintain their existing economic base. That is, communities must use their current human, social, institutional, and physical resources to build a self-sustaining economic system.

It is often asked, by persons concerned with this new wave of local economic planning, whether this activity merely represents a new approach or if it is the reformulation of the failed "trickle down" policies of the past. The key issue is whether this new version of local or community-based economic development is genuinely better and more effective than past efforts. Can local governments and/or neighborhoods, working together or separately, create new jobs? More important (and perhaps more fundamental), are these new ap-proaches just moving the existing jobs around the nation with give-aways and gimmicks? Is it, in fact, possible to generate more work and more "good" jobs in a technology-based economy? If local efforts can generate employment, are these efforts cost-effective? Or is it

Edward J. Blakely, *Planning Local Economic Development: Theory and Practice*, pp. 57–70, copyright 1989 by Sage Publications. Reprinted by permission of Sage Publications, Inc.

inevitable that local institutions are only playing at the margins of the employment-generation process without making any substantial impact on the real requirements for employment in a transitional economy? Can the job-formation process be related to the people who need the work? Is it inevitable that the "underclass," the racial minorities, women, and other disadvantaged persons, will not share in the benefits of any form of economic development, be it local or otherwise? Is economic development another code term for corporate control of community assets? Finally, at what cost to planning, zoning, and environmental considerations is local employment being pursued?

These are difficult questions. This article provides a link between the existing theories of regional growth and decline, to forge an operational paradigm for engaging in local economic development. The conceptual framework for local economic development emerges from basic development theories. This article is not a review of all development theories but aims at providing an intersection for the public policies that are the basis for local economic development.

Defining local economic development

Locally based economic development is not merely new rhetoric but represents a fundamental shift in the actors as well as the activities associated with economic development. It is essentially a process by which local government and/or community-based groups manage their existing resources and enter into new partnership arrangements with the private sector, or with each other, to create new jobs and stimulate economic activity in a well-defined economic zone. The central feature in locally oriented or based economic development is in the emphasis on "endogenous development" policies using the potential of local human, institutional, and physical resources. This orientation leads to a focus on taking local initiatives in the development process to create new employment and stimulate increased economic activity. The reasons for this are as follows:

[Previous economic development theories and program efforts] . . . have relied too heavily on a belief that the benefits of economic growth and expansion will "trickle down" to improve conditions of the poor. . . . They have separated macroeconomic policies and maintenance programs into two separate and distinct camps; and . . . they have focused almost exclusively on trying to remedy perceived "defects" in the poor—inadequate education or skills, weak community supports, lack of motivation—and ignored the very real, potent barriers in the structure of opportunities the poor confront on the "demand" side of the labor market equation.[1]

Local economic development is process oriented. That is, it is a process involving the formation of new institutions, the development of alternative industries, the improvement in the capacity of existing employers to produce better products, the identification of new markets, the transfer of knowledge, and the nurturing of new firms and enterprises. As Williams, writing for the OECD, puts it,

When you move beyond importing [jobs] . . . and start a strategy of creative innovation and adaptation, then [local] "innovation" becomes an economic, social, and a local [development] preoccupation, rather than just a technical one.[2]

No matter what form it takes, local economic development has one primary goal, which is to increase the number and variety of job opportunities available to local people. In performing these activities, local governments and/or community groups must take on an initiating, rather than a passive, role.

In essence, local government—with community participation and using the resources of existing community-based institutions (where they exist and possess economic potential)—is required to assess the potentials and marshal the necessary resources to design and develop the local economy. Local government and community organizations are realizing that *all* public sector actions have an impact upon private decisions. Even the most narrow local governments, perhaps restricting their activities to the traditional housekeeping services, have affected economic development in their communities, if only through their passivity. Many local governments have probably acted unwittingly to restrict employment opportunities without understanding or assessing the economic consequences of their actions. Similarly, neighborhood-level community institutions, both nonprofit and public, have had dramatic impacts on private investment. Neighborhoods with active churches and neighborhood organizations that work toward the constructive development of their community act as beacons to developers and investors. Further, good community schools, both public and private, are essential factors in the potential location of new businesses. Private decisions and public economic activity are intimately related and affect employment opportunities for all local residents. This concept should lead local governments and community-based organizations to take a new and different perspective toward planned, coordinated development initiatives. Communities large and small need to understand that, no matter how depressed or wealthy they are, local government, community institutions, and the private sector are essential partners in the economic development process.

Theories of growth and development

Currently, no theory or set of theories adequately explains regional or local economic development. There are several partial theories that can help us understand the underlying rationale for local economic development. The sum of these theories may be expressed as

Local/regional development = *f*(natural resources, labor, capital investment, entrepreneurship, transport, communication, industrial
composition, technology, size, export market, international economic situation, local government capacity, national government and state spending,
and development supports)

All of these factors may be important but it is the segregation
of each of them into their component parts that forms the basis for
development theory and local economic actions.

The role of neoclassical economic theory   Neoclassical economic
theory does not have a significant spatial dimension. Nonetheless,
neoclassical models of large-scale economic systems can be applied
to the competitive positioning and wealth generation of a subarea of
a larger economy.

The neoclassical theory offers two major concepts to regional
and local development: equilibrium and mobility. These concepts
provide that all economic systems will reach a natural equilibrium if
capital can flow without restriction. That is, capital will flow from
high-wage/cost to low-wage/cost areas, because the latter offer a
higher return on investment. In local development terms, this
means that ghettos should draw capital because prices for property
and sometimes labor fall to meet the demand of the marketplace. If
the model worked perfectly, then all areas would gradually reach a
state of equal status in the economic system. Much of this rationale
underlies the current wave of deregulation of banking, airlines, util-
ities, and similar services. In theory, all areas can compete in a de-
regulated market.

In a similar manner, advocates of neoclassical theory would oppose any community regulations on the movement of firms from one
area of the nation to another, or even offshore. Neoclassical theorists oppose moves by community groups and local governments
that might place restrictions on firm locations, such as minority or
local equity participation. They suggest that such moves are
doomed to fail and disrupt the normal and necessary movement of
capital. Moreover, neoclassical advocates argue that there should be
no attempts to save dying or uncompetitive firms. Further, they argue that workers who lose their jobs should move to new employment areas as a further stimulus to development in such places.
Among regional and local economic development advocates, there
are many detractors of neoclassical theories and the policies derived
from them because of the anti-intervention stance of neoclassical
economists. In addition, neoclassical models tell us little about the
real reasons some areas are competitive and others fail. Further,
the neoclassical framework is generally viewed as antagonistic to
the interest of communities as places with a raison d'être beyond
their economic utility.

On the other hand, there are useful concepts that can be derived from the neoclassical position. First, in a market society, all communities must ensure that they use their resources in a manner that attracts capital. Artificial barriers, inferior governmental bureaucracy, and an absence of a "good business climate" are, in fact, barriers to economic development. Second, communities or disadvantaged neighborhoods can and should argue for the resources necessary to assist them to reach an equilibrium status with surrounding areas. This can be partially accomplished by upgrading commercial properties, through local government loans and grants, as well as by offering training and other programs that enhance the value of local labor. These measures can act as inducements that equalize the value of inner-city neighborhoods and other disadvantaged areas with more prosperous places.

Economic base theory   As stated previously, communities are socioeconomic systems. As whole systems, they trade with other communities outside their boundaries. Adherents of economic base theory postulate that the determinants for economic growth are directly related to the demand for goods, services, and products from other areas outside the local economic boundaries of the community. In essence, the growth of industries that use local resources, including labor and materials for final export elsewhere, will generate both local wealth and jobs.

The local economic development strategies that emerge from this theory emphasize the importance of aid to businesses that have a national or international market above and beyond aid to local service firms. Implementation of this model would include measures that reduce barriers to export-based firms establishing themselves in an area, with such measures providing, for instance, tax relief, transport facilities, and telecommunications. Moreover, firm recruitment and economic assistance efforts would be aimed at supporting or encouraging export-oriented enterprises.

Many of the current entrepreneurial and high-technology strategies aimed at attracting or generating new firms are also based on economic base models. The rationale is that nonexport firms or service-providing businesses will develop automatically to supply export firms or the population that works in them. Moreover, it is argued that export industries have higher job multipliers than local service firms. Thus every job created in an export firm will generate, depending on the sector, several jobs elsewhere in the economy. There are regional economic methods that will test and measure such impacts of firms on the local economy.

The weakness in this model is that it is based on external demand rather than internal need. Overzealous application of base models can lead to a skewed economy almost entirely dependent upon external, global, or national market forces. This model is, however, useful in determining the balance between industrial types and sectors that a community needs to develop for economic stability.

Location theory   There is an old saying among regional economists to the effect that there are only three important variables in regional growth. They are location, location, and location! There is some logic to this statement with respect to industrial site development. Firms tend to minimize their cost by selecting locations that maximize their opportunities to reach the marketplace. The old industrial/manufacturing model postulated that the best location was almost always on the cheapest transport link between raw materials and markets.

There are other obvious variables that affect the quality or suitability of a location, such as labor cost, the cost of energy, availability of suppliers, communications, education and training facilities, local government quality and responsiveness, and sanitation. Different firms require differing mixes of these factors in order to be competitive. Therefore, communities generally attempt to manipulate the cost of several of these factors to become attractive to industrial firms. All of these actions are taken to enhance a *location* beyond its natural attributes.

The limitation of location theory today is that modern technology and telecommunications alter the significance of specific locations for the production and distribution of goods. In many respects, almost any community can compete as an urban center now because transportation cost for the most sophisticated products has been reduced dramatically. Moreover, less tangible variables, such as the quality of community life, now seem to overshadow the obvious advantages of large market or natural resource areas.

The contribution of location theory to local economic development is in the realistic parameters it places on the development process. Communities need to ascertain the relative value of their locational attributes with the other combination of resources that the area possesses.

Central place theory   The basic concept underlying central place theory is that there is a hierarchy of places. Each urban center is supported by a series of smaller places that provide both resources (industries and raw materials) that require a central clearinghouse to filter into the world marketplace. Regional development models for rural areas have relied heavily on central place theory to guide resource allocations among country centers, the thesis being that the development of a central country center of larger-scale population would improve the economic well-being of the entire region.

The application of central place theory can be seen in the early work of the Tennessee Valley Authority (TVA), Rural Electrification, Economic Development Administration (EDA), and similar rural service bureaucracies. Each of these organizations attempted to develop a regional economic plan with one or two communities either designated or emerging as regional nodes for development.

There is a relevant application of central place theory for local economic development for both rural and urban places. For example, it is necessary to differentiate the functions of various neighborhood areas for them to remain viable centers. Some areas will become region-serving while others will serve only the resident community. Local economic development specialists can assist communities or neighborhoods to develop their functional role in the regional economic system.

Cumulative causation theories   Casual observation of the decay of urban neighborhoods demonstrates the basic concepts of the cumulative causation thesis: The interplay of market forces increases rather than decreases the inequality between areas. As a result, a divergence in regional income is a predictable outcome. Market forces, by their nature, pull capital, skill, and expertise to certain areas. These areas accumulate a large-scale competitive advantage over the rest of the system. Myrdal expounded this theory and described it in the following manner:

Suppose accidental change occurs in a community, and it is not immediately cancelled out in a stream of events; for example, a factory employing a large part of the population burns down . . . and cannot be rebuilt economically, at least not at that locality. The immediate effect is that the firm owning it goes out of business and its workers become unemployed. This will decrease income and demand. In its turn, the decreased demand will lower incomes and cause unemployment in all sorts of other businesses in the community which sold to or served the firm and its employees. . . .

   If there are no exogenous changes, the community will be less tempting for outside businesses and workers who had contemplated moving in. As the process gathers momentum, businesses established in the community and workers living there will increasingly find reasons for moving out in order to seek better markets somewhere else. This will again decrease income and demand.[3]

These "backwash effects" prevent low-income neighborhoods from developing the requisite internal capacity for revitalization. On the other hand, the growth of prosperous areas tends to feed on itself if the growth-inducing factors remain conducive. As a result, less-well-off areas, be they rural backward regions or inner-city ghettos, tend to send their capital and labor supply to better places without any significant return. It is for this reason that many advocates of ghetto capitalism propose the movement of jobs into the neighborhoods rather than the movement of people away from their communities in search of work. In addition, the loss of community retail banks, supermarkets, and commercial establishments continually drains both rural underdeveloped areas and ghettos of the requnite internal capital for rebuilding themselves.

The community development corporations and rural development centers are one response to creating new institutional arrangements to rebuild underserved communities. These organizations are attempting to restore the market, and act as capital retainers or capital attractors for areas where market forces are especially weak.

Of course, the weakness of this theory is in its application to small areas, such as urban inner-city ghettos. It is difficult to obtain data that shows capital leakage even when it is observable. Further, it is extremely difficult to know where to intervene in a decaying neighborhood economy. Do you reestablish banks or supermarkets? Given that ghetto markets are poor in both money and use of funds, how do you accumulate any reinvestment capital? These are very difficult questions that local economic developers need to consider before they embark on attempting to improve very troubled areas. In a sense, every cause is an effect.

Attraction models   Industrial attraction theory is the economic development model most widely used by all communities. The basic economic theory that underlies attraction is that a community can alter its market position with industrialists by offering incentives and subsidies. The assumption is that any public or private subsidies provided will be recouped by the increased economic wealth and taxes generated by the new activity. A more cynical view, supported by considerable evidence, is that the cost of such efforts is paid by the workers and taxpayers of the community.[4]

Communities are products. As such, they must be "packaged" and appropriately displayed. The objective evidence of this packaging of communities can be observed in magazine and newspaper advertisements extolling the virtues of certain places over others. There is some cynicism with regard to this mode of economic development. Nonetheless, there is considerable anecdotal evidence that community promotion works and that the failure to use it may be a political liability.

A new approach in attraction is the change in emphasis from attracting factories to one of attracting the entrepreneurial population, particularly certain socioeconomic groups, to a community or area. New middle-class migrants to an area bring both buying power and the capability to attract employers. In addition, recent migrants are more likely to start new firms. As a result, many communities have reassessed their firm attraction efforts and reoriented them toward "people" attraction. This approach has been particularly effective in rural areas where the quality-of-life factor has attracted new populations. This, in turn, has led to increased economic growth as a response to both internal demand and new export enterprises created by the new migrants.

Finally, the attraction model underlies some of the current emphasis on "civic entrepreneurism." The notion is that nations, states, and communities can become attractive places for entrepreneurs to flourish. A corollary theory has emerged that suggests that some localities offer special "knowledge networks" and act as incubators for high-technology firms or inventors. These areas are natural entrepreneurial centers because they develop a certain style or esprit de corps. Route 128 in Massachusetts, the Silicon Valley, and the North Carolina Triangle, as well as some areas of Florida, have gained reputations as innovation centers.

Communities all over the world are beginning to initiate policies and programs to make their area more attractive to investors, firms, new migrants, entrepreneurs, and others. The theoretical basis for this activity is that places can display themselves and offer incentives that give them a *competitive advantage* over other areas with similar resource endowments. The extent to which all these efforts cancel one another out or provide businesses with unnecessary and expensive incentives is a topic of considerable debate.

This approach suggests, however, that no city or neighborhood should hide its virtues "under a bushel basket." Some form of marketing is necessary; the means and the rationale are as important as the desired result in undertaking this mode of development planning, given that the ends may not always justify the means.

Toward a synthetic theory of local economic development

Existing development theory is an insufficient template for local economic development activities. Therefore, an alternative approach to development theory is formulated here to serve as a context for local economic development planning and action. The approach advanced here is a synthesis and reformulation of existing concepts. It serves as a basis for thinking about and taking action within the local economic development context.

Employment   The major, and sometimes the sole, rationale for communities to engage in active development efforts is to boost local employment. In the neoclassical formulation, the inducement of lower wage rates and cheaper costs is sufficient to create employment. Two implications flow from this formulation. One is to change the quality of the place, that is, to provide special locational incentives. The other one is to increase the value of the local labor force.

The myriad job training and job development schemes in this

country are testimony to the importance attached to transforming existing labor into a more useful product for existing employers. The enterprise zone is a direct example of attempts to stimulate job creation for a specific population by altering the value of locations.

The goal of local economic development is not to alter but to enhance the value of people and places. The conceptual position taken is that employment development is a function of how the community builds economic opportunities that "fit" the human resources and utilize/maximize the existing natural and institutional resource base. In essence, the emphasis shifts from the demand (firm) side of the equation to the supply (labor and natural resources) side as the conceptual framework for formulating development solutions.

Development base   The economic base model relies heavily on a sectoral approach to economic development. Transactions within the economic system dominate this approach rather than the failures and inadequacies of the economic system in which the transactions are taking place. Within this context, the inputs and outputs of the economic system move well beyond the economic interchanges, and the model examines institutional and other linkages that make the system work.

Local economic development theory starts with a premise that the institutional base must form a major component of both finding the problems in the local economy and altering institutional arrangements. Building new institutional relationships is the new substance of economic development. Communities can take control of their destiny when and if they assemble the resources and information necessary to build their own future. This is not a closed political process but an open one that places local citizens in a position to plan and manage their own economic destiny.

Location assets   Technology is shattering the traditional view of physical location as the major determinant of development. Firms, even large-scale manufacturing operations, are not as stable as they have been. No one knows precisely what is "footloose" with regard to locational criteria. Thus the old view that the availability of transportation and market systems would determine a community's economic viability is outdated.

Moreover, while heretofore, rural communities had spent most of their energy in attempting to acquire roads and related infrastructure to promote development, they now find that this thrust is insufficient. Some rural areas are growing even without such large-scale investment. It does not seem to matter whether a rural community is a designated growth center with regard to population or industrial development.

Location, by itself, is no longer a "pull" factor. In some respects, urban and particularly inner-city locations represent "push" factors. Both firms and people want to avoid these places because their image is unattractive. Crime and associated issues make it difficult to do business in many urban environments. Lack of cultural and educational facilities can retard the development of many rural communities.

The new local economic development model suggests that there are *location inducing* factors. These factors apply more to the quality of the local physical and social environment than to larger-scale geographic considerations. Moreover, developing a community's recreational, housing, and social institutions is an important determinant of economic viability. Concentrating on building the social and institutional network creates the *inducing environment* for a firm to develop or locate in a community. In essence, if the structure is organized in the correct manner, economic activity will ensue and it will not have to be pursued.

Knowledge resources   Research resources are the base for economic development in a "knowledge intensive" world economy. In the modern economy, information, more than goods, is exchanged. The development of new information in, for example, biotechnology, computing, and telecommunications is of enormous value. As a result, the loci of economic innovation and product development have moved from the field to the laboratory.

Major research universities, research institutes, and research units in business and industry are of enormous significance to a local economy. Therefore, localities must develop ways to tap the intellectual resource centers of their region or area. These intellectual resources can be of major assistance in developing new goods and services or unlocking the potential of existing natural and other resources.

The quality of an area's human resource base is a major inducement to all industries. If the local human resource base is substantial, new firms will be created by it irrespective of location, or else existing firms will migrate there. Therefore, communities must not only build jobs to fit the existing populace, they must also build institutions that expand the capability of this population. Rural communities and inner-city neighborhoods seldom have higher education or research institutions that service them. Indeed, the rural communities and urban neighborhoods seldom consider the need for such resources beyond the teaching function or community problem-solving requirement. Local economic development, however, both now and in the near future, will be dependent upon the ability of communities to use the resources of higher education and research-related institutions. Rather than attracting a new factory that may initially employ thousands, a community is better served by attract-

Table 1. Toward a theory of local economic development.

Component	Old concept	New concept
Employment	More firms = more jobs	Firms that build quality jobs that fit the local population
Development base	Building economic sectors	Building new economic institutions
Location assets	Comparative advantage based on physical assets	Competitive advantage based on quality environment
Knowledge resource	Available work force	Knowledge as economic generator

ing and retaining a few small, related research labs in leading-edge technologies that will eventually create jobs and stability for the total region.

The emerging framework

A new conceptual framework is emerging to serve as the parameter for local economic development (see Table 1). It does not enjoy any status yet. The basic tenets of this framework suggest that local economic development is a process that emphasizes the full use of existing human and natural resources to build employment and create wealth within a defined locality.

1. Corporation for Enterprise Development, *Investing in Poor Communities* (Washington, D.C.: Corporation for Enterprise Development, April 1982), 2.
2. Rt. Hon. S. Williams, *Local Employment Generation: The Need for Innovation, Information, and Suitable Technology* (Paris: Organization for Economic Cooperation and Development, 1986), 1.
3. G. Myrdal, *Economic Theory and Underdeveloped Regions* (London: Duckworth Press, 1957), 23.
4. Barry Bluestone, Bennett Harrison, and Lawrence Baker, *Corporate Flight: The Causes and Consequences of Economic Dislocation* (Washington, D.C.: Progressive Alliance Books, 1981).

The Power of Manufacturing Networks

C. Richard Hatch

The overall competitiveness of American industry has come to rest squarely on the ability of existing small and medium-sized firms to meet the cost, quality, and delivery demands of major industrial customers. These smaller companies, which employ nearly two-thirds of the blue-collar labor force, now supply the bulk of the parts and components used in the production of finished goods for both domestic and export markets.

The proliferation of small manufacturing firms and the downscaling of big ones are creating significant challenges for economic development officials. It is one thing to negotiate the location of a branch manufacturing plant employing several thousand workers. It is quite another to service thousands of smaller enterprises in hundreds of different industries, each with specific technologies and markets to be mastered. Yet, as firm size goes down, the need for such assistance goes up; the traditional limitations of small firms—restricted access to capital, little or no R&D capability, lack of management depth and marketing savvy—are well known. The magnitude of the problem, the limited time remaining to reach competitive levels, and the shortage of public resources are driving home the need for new approaches.

Reprinted by permission of the author, C. Richard Hatch, Manufacturing Network Project, Center for Manufacturing Systems, New Jersey Institute of Technology, 12 Engle Street, Englewood, New Jersey 07631. The article was published in the Winter 1991 issue of *transAtlantic Perspectives*, a publication of the German Marshall Fund of the United States. Portions of it were originally published by the Corporation For Enterprise Development in "Manufacturing Modernization: Strategies That Don't Work, Strategies That Do," *Entrepreneurial Economy Review* (Autumn 1990) and in *Flexible Manufacturing Networks: Cooperation for Competitiveness in a Global Economy* (1989).

Fortunately, the stewards of our state and city economies can turn to the prosperous small-firm economies of Europe for effective models. In southwestern Germany, inter-firm cooperation has greatly increased innovation and productivity in the textile machinery, automotive component, and electronics sectors. Denmark's furniture, apparel, and electronics industries are regaining their competitive edge in like fashion. And in Italy close-knit subcontracting networks permit very small companies to dominate sectors which at first glance appear more suited to large-scale production. One of the keys is the propensity of firms in these regions to link their complementary skills and share the costs of doing business in manufacturing networks.

A manufacturing network is a group of firms that cooperate in order to compete—that collaborate to achieve together what each cannot alone. In networks, groups of independent companies can share overhead, access expensive technologies, and blend complementary capabilities to bring innovative products to new markets.

Networks coalesce around common needs and opportunities. Through participation in *service networks* dozens or even hundreds of firms share the costs of market forecasting, quality certification, materials purchasing, or financial management. Out of them blossom many *production networks*, in which a few or many small companies cooperate to exploit niche markets.

Emilia-Romagna: Epicenter of the network system

The industrial model incorporating both types of networks emerged first in north-central Italy in the region of Emilia-Romagna, where bitter labor-management struggles in the late 1960s cut productivity and curtailed large firms' ability to respond to market shifts. The oil shocks of the 1970s and skyrocketing Third World debt hit the biggest employers—the farm machinery makers—particularly hard. At the same time, foreign competitors were making serious inroads into the traditional markets of the region's apparel and shoe producers.

Even so, over the next dozen years the explosive growth of small enterprises in the region's principal cities—Bologna, Modena, Reggio, Parma, Carpi—paralleled the steep loss of mass production jobs. The key was the spread of manufacturing networks. Out of necessity, the regional government, in collaboration with labor and trade associations, learned how to foster cooperating systems of small and medium-sized firms, bringing them together around shared services until strong commercial ties could give them a life of their own.

In Carpi, for example, economist Loredana Ligabue conceived a plan to provide vital management services to knitwear firms, and she arranged for financial backing, first from the European Community's Social Fund and then from the regional government. Her description of the creation of the "network hub" called CITER is instructive:

"I talked first to firm owners. On the basis of the problems and opportunities we identified, we set up CITER to help move the Carpi knitwear industry to a higher plane. First, we worked on product change—higher fashion—so that we could ask higher prices. Second, we had to introduce new technologies to fill the niche we had chosen. Third, we needed to expand our markets and move away from dependence on Germany. We gathered the best market information from around the world (at prices individual firms couldn't afford), organized trade missions, disseminated information—all of these things done always in groups."

Today CITER provides sophisticated international fashion forecasting and technical services to more than 600 dues-paying member firms. None of the little firms in the Carpi knitwear district could afford even one of the expensive consultants readily available in Manhattan or Milan, but 600 of them together are able to access the very best services.

In the Emilia-Romagna region's dense industrial districts, small firms routinely combine resources to produce and export machine tools, automatic machinery, motorcycles, automobiles, electronic controls, agricultural equipment, ceramic tiles, furniture, shoes, knitwear, and clothing of all kinds. The owners of these firms describe themselves in quite the same terms used by their American counterparts: they are fiercely individualistic and highly competitive. They vie for positions in the best networks, not because they are culturally attuned to cooperation, but because they are always on the lookout for ways to enter new markets or increase margins. As a result, in ten years, the region of Emilia-Romagna has moved to the top in national income rankings and to eighth position in all of Europe, putting it on par with high Scandinavian levels and well above any region of the United States.

To some early observers, it seemed that Emilia-Romagna's little firms might simply have found a few fortuitous niches. It is now clear that, in fact, aided by professionally staffed trade associations and decentralized sectoral service centers, they have created a system of production that fits precisely with the forces that are reshaping manufacturing worldwide. The onset of narrowly segmented markets and arrival of computerized production systems have greatly magnified the difficulties faced by larger companies whose management practices and technological choices often inhibit rapid innovation and efficient small-batch manufacturing—the forte of network firms.

Denmark: Overcoming the limitations of size

In Denmark, too, many small firms have gotten engaged in networks because this kind of collaboration contributes measurably to

the bottom line. A country of five million people facing the impend-
ing single European market with most of its blue-collar workers in
very small firms, Denmark launched a national network program in
1989.

The Ministry of Industry set aside $140 million over three years
for industrial modernization, export promotion, and network development. As a first step, key industry consultants from both public
and private sectors were run through an intensive training course
to become "network brokers." In the course, potential brokers
learned how to organize competing firms, spot mutual business opportunities, assess modernization needs, and coordinate group services.

At the same time, a multiphase program of challenge grants
was announced. Phase One offered groups of firms up to $7,500 to
conduct network feasibility studies. To apply, only a simple letter
signed by three or more firms was required. Later phases have provided larger grants for long-term group projects such as production
coordination systems, export marketing, and new product development.

The initial outreach to business included direct mailings to
every manufacturer in the country, full-page newspaper ads, regional conferences co-hosted with trade associations—even televi-
sion talk shows.

Last July the Danish government announced that the Network
Program "had taken on a life of its own and become self-propelling."
In one year, 3,000 companies had been catalyzed into active participation. The strategic alliances they have formed are giving them the
critical mass they need to develop a diversified array of new products for export—from hotel furnishings to integrated diagnostic
equipment to turnkey golf courses.

The Network Program is changing two things in Denmark—
two things that must also change in the United States. The first is
the way government delivers services to industry, and the second is
business culture itself. Instead of deciding what business needs and
staffing a project to provide it, the Danish Ministry is saying, "Manufacturers, define your problems. Tell us in which markets you wish
to compete and how we can help you do it well—for your benefit and
that of the country as a whole." At the same time, the owners and
managers of Danish companies are being encouraged to change the
way they think about the balance between cooperation and competition. Increasingly, they are turning to one another for the knowledge, skills, and support needed to adopt new technologies and compete successfully in the single global marketplace.

Working principles for a network strategy

The Danish and Italian efforts to strengthen the small-firm manufacturing sector contain important lessons for the United States. In

fact, a constant set of principles guides economic development policy in Europe's network regions from Sweden's Småland to Baden-Württemberg to Barcelona and Bologna. They are also being applied with good results in fledgling American initiatives.

The profit incentive principle European regions drive modernization by identifying profitable business opportunities for local firms. The entrepreneurial energy they arouse in those firms and among local innovators is channeled into discussions about "best practice" manufacturing methods—creating a taste for advanced technologies. This is the reverse of the usual U.S. practice which *first* transfers technology to the firms, and *then* hopes that the new capabilities will eventually find a market outlet. But this is changing. Following the European approach, Maine, Mississippi, West Virginia, and Michigan have recently entered into a compact to develop a "market observatory" for their rural manufacturing companies. Through it they will harness the profit motive to help speed the adoption of modern manufacturing methods, along with the diversification of mature industry sectors.

The efficiency principle States must learn to stretch their investments if they are to reach thousands of firms in the next few years. No government has the resources to do this using the direct supplier route, "selling" its services to one firm at a time. But government can, in effect, wholesale quality assistance to groups of firms. The Michigan Modernization Service, for example, learning from European experience, is working closely with local trade associations, responding to needs their members identify. It also has begun to bring individual client firms together around common interests in training, marketing, and technological innovation.

The principle of (maximum feasible) participation The best way to get industry involved in continuous modernization is to put it in charge of the process. This shift of focus in service planning and delivery—from supply-side to demand-side—is the central lesson Italy's recent industrial renaissance offers us. Customer participation is currently the subject of key U.S. experiments here, as Ohio, Arkansas, Michigan, North Carolina, and Maine use challenge grants to motivate firms to come together, build their capacity to articulate needs, and define solutions. In doing so, these states are taking the first steps in creating powerful relationships for long-term competitiveness.

The principle of sustainability U.S. states tend to offer industry assistance free of charge. Because financial resources are limited, programs remain small. Collecting fees for service could help good programs grow. European modernization efforts often start with low

U.S. firms turning to networks in pursuit of competitiveness

The power of the network to help small firms apply new technology, improve product quality, and enter and succeed in new, faraway markets may soon be seriously tested in the United States. Consider as evidence:

In Chehalis, Washington, 200 small wood-product manufacturers are banding together to market their products jointly in retail outlets. Their joint design efforts are meant to lead to the creation of complementary lines of furniture and accessories, all made from local wood species. Other forms of cooperation, such as common use of a kiln, are also being explored.

Further north, on the Olympic Peninsula, a production network could emerge in response to concerns about shrinking timber supplies. Primary and secondary wood-product manufacturers in Port Townsend and surrounding communities are assessing joint manufacturing opportunities as one possible approach to stabilizing wood supplies within their small region.

In Montana, a new network links diverse manufacturing enterprises owned by seven Indian tribes. At present, these operations mainly serve protected Department of Defense markets, and the tribes are eager to see them succeed in nonprotected commercial markets. The network is being asked to clarify the principal technological, marketing, and training barriers to be overcome.

On the Minnesota-Dakota border, forty firms have incorporated the Tri-State Manufacturers Association to help one another modernize and diversify and to preserve their rural communities. TSMA's first project, done in conjunction with a local technical college, was a course in total quality management for workers and managers.

fees and raise them gradually as new services demonstrably contribute to profits. This practice not only uses price mechanisms to ensure that services are client-driven, but sets each program on a financial path that will eventually make it self-sustaining.

The principle of cooperation   In the American business culture, individual companies are expected to cope by themselves with the massive changes occurring in the competitive environment. Regardless of size, U.S. firms must independently manage worker training, procurement, manufacturing operations, R&D, marketing, and sales.

One reason more and more foreign manufacturing economies are gaining on us is that they are fostering a different kind of industrial system, one in which cooperation forms the basis for competitive success. In Italy, Denmark, Japan, and other countries, public sector agencies and trade associations actively promote interdependent relationships among firms. In the process, they have created the *group clients* for public sector services that the efficiency prin-

Fall River and New Bedford, Massachusetts, apparel contractors formed the Needle Trades Action Project five years ago to stem further erosion of their industry. Their cooperative efforts in market development, skill training, and day care have improved the quality of work life as well as firm productivity.

Six metal fabricating firms in central Maine are working to design, produce, and market a new type of road sanding device that has serious export potential. Further north, machinery manufacturers have set up a shared computer-aided design station with a grant from the state's Science and Technology Commission. Individually too small to afford the cost of a skilled operator, these firms have increased their competitiveness by sharing staff and technology.

The Machine Action Project organizes metalworking firms in the Springfield, Massachusetts, area. Beginning with an innovative apprenticeship program that has brought women and minorities into the industry, MAP has moved on to create interfirm computer links to facilitate joint bidding and group manufacturing.

A dozen heat treat firms in Ohio have forged an alliance with the state's Edison Materials Technology Center. Their job is to organize the entire sector (more than 100 small companies). In return they will have access to the technology resources of the Center and several universities—in effect a collective R&D division for the entire sector.

In the Florida Panhandle, five defense industry subcontractors got the message from a network conference sponsored by the Southern Technology Council. Now they market their combined capabilities—and have penetrated new, high-value-added markets.

ciple demands. In line with the principles of sustainability, participation, and cooperation, the networks they have helped to form are always market-driven and industry-led.

First step for any state: Recruit brokers

Projects under way in a dozen U.S. states demonstrate the receptivity of American business to network strategies (see sidebar). But a few model networks cannot measurably affect regional wealth or national competitiveness. Thousands more are needed.

Faced with the need to move swiftly on modernization, any state's first step is to recruit knowledgeable and trusted individuals—from state agencies, local economic development organizations, trade associations, community colleges, and university extension projects—for training as network brokers. In the process of helping manufacturing firms help themselves, the broker has well-established tasks.

Get them talking. Establish regular communication among firms, and between firms and those with whom they need to cooperate—

business service providers, labor unions, marketing specialists, product designers, university laboratories, equipment manufacturers, and customers.

Deploy skills, not firms. View firms as "packets of skill and equipment" that can be deployed, in changing network combinations, in response to market signals. For example, when a hanger manufacturer is seen as a plastic injection molder, and a breadbox maker as a metal-forming firm, it is possible to envision forms of cooperation that could move them into new markets.

Spot common needs. Identify critical problems for sector competitiveness through constant contact with firms and their markets. Common needs are the basis for collective solutions.

Work toward hubs. Turn what is learned about obstacles to growth into specialized services—services that no small firm could possibly afford except through network participation. These crucial collective services will be the hubs around which network cooperation coalesces.

   In this era of rapid technological change and fierce competition, many American manufacturers are at risk. Given the need to modernize thousands of small firms in a short time, state governments would be well advised to concentrate their resources on coordinating services to groups of firms, providing strategic information on growing markets, and catalyzing manufacturing networks. This will require a reorientation of state economic development policies and a new emphasis on helping U.S. manufacturing firms help themselves.

   With forceful state leadership, business-government collaboration and network cooperation could expand fast enough and broadly enough to protect our existing endowment of manufacturing firms and, on that base, rebuild a thriving industrial economy.

PART 2

Economic
Foundations

Developing an Internationally Competitive Workforce

William E. Nothdurft

Almost since it began, the Council of State Policy and Planning Agencies [now the Council of Governors' Policy Advisors] has focused much of its research attention on strengthening state capacity for economic development. In part as a result, many states today have highly sophisticated economic development departments that are themselves sources of policy and program innovation.

But several months of studying first hand the economic strategies currently being pursued by several European nations as they organize to confront the 1992 Single European Market has led me to a conclusion that, I would argue, has sweeping implications for states. It is not so much a new conclusion as it is a reinforced one. It is this: *State Departments of Economic Development can create the most enlightened and advanced development strategies in the nation and still fail the test of competitiveness, unless their programs are backed up by equally enlightened and advanced workforce education and training programs—because the challenge of competitiveness is fundamentally a challenge of competence.*

During the past decade, while many of us have been scrutinizing the Japanese, the advanced industrial nations of Western Europe have quietly pulled themselves out of the doldrums and into the forefront of the global economic competition. In West Germany, Sweden, France, Italy, even Great Britain, long called "the sick man

William E. Nothdurft is an independent public policy consultant based in Bethesda, Maryland. This article, based upon work funded by the German Marshall Fund of the United States, is the text of a presentation made at the annual meeting of the Council of State Policy and Planning Agencies [now the Council of Governors' Policy Advisors], Monterey, California, August 1989. Reprinted with permission.

of Europe," productivity has soared, employment has risen, personal income has grown, and exports have increased steadily.

But although these countries have developed highly innovative economic development policies—flexible manufacturing networks and self-employment schemes, among many others—they are competitive principally because they are committed to creating a continuous stream of well-educated, highly skilled workers. We have failed to make the same commitment, and our economies are suffering as a result. Even in the Northeast, in the midst of an historically robust economy, welfare caseloads are persistently high even as the number of pages of want ads in local newspapers exceed the pages devoted to news. People and jobs are *both* going begging.

One cause of this situation is the educational system itself: the failure of secondary schools to keep young people engaged in schoolwork and to provide them with the kind of educational and skill credentials that enable them to move smoothly into the workforce, and a chaotic vocational education and job-training system that often has little connection to the world of work. Even for those who go on to college, the path between school and work is haphazard; for those who do not go on to college, or who are burdened with other handicaps, the path is often invisible.

But there are demographic reasons as well: The postwar baby boom is over and the entry of women to the workforce has begun to peak. Over the next ten years, more than half of all new workers will be immigrant and non-white men and women—that is, minorities will be the majority. And this emerging workforce approaches the world of work with significant educational and skill handicaps.

Meanwhile, at the same time that the education and skill levels of the workforce are dropping, the knowledge and skill requirements of the job market are increasing rapidly.

This mismatch is our economic Achilles' heel. Create all the economic development programs you wish; if you do not correct this mismatch, economic development will fail.

Allan Larsson, Director General of Sweden's National Labor Market Board (and lately a consultant to Michigan's Department of Commerce) is fond of saying: "We must create not a 'high tech' but a 'high skill' economy, through competence-building at all levels of education and business."

This commitment to competence-building is the key to the economic success of Sweden, West Germany, and several other European nations, and it holds some important lessons as you seek to strengthen your economic development programs. Consider the programs under way in three European nations with very different political and economic philosophies:

Sweden's public education system begins introducing children to the world of work by the second grade. By the time they reach upper secondary school, young people will have chosen from among more than 400 lines of study aiming at credential-building in a specific trade or line of work. By their final year of secondary school, these students may spend as much as 60 percent of their school day working in a specific industry and putting the finishing touches on their work skills. 90 percent of Sweden's young people go through this process; the balance are given special attention and gently guided to a course of study and skill-building that suits them. Once in the labor force, a national employment service links them with jobs and a nationwide, but private, training company assures them that they can always upgrade or alter their skills. Education and training curricula are developed jointly with employers and labor unions and all employers participate in the employment service.

West Germany has the world's best developed apprenticeship program—called the "dual system" because it is jointly operated by industry and the vocational education system of every German *Land* or state. Like the Swedes, German children are introduced to the world of work at an early age. By the equivalent of the 10th grade, roughly 80 percent of these young people will enter the Dual System. They will choose from among hundreds of occupations, acquire an apprenticeship in a private company in their chosen field, and spend the next three years developing skills—four days a week on the job to gain practical skills and one day a week in a local vocational school to gain theoretical skills. Industry-run Chambers of Commerce operate their own schools to ensure that young people apprenticing in small shops receive as broad an education as those in bigger and better-equipped factories. The partnership between business and public education is long-standing and carefully protected.

Great Britain, with perhaps the weakest workforce in Europe, embarked several years ago on a multi-billion dollar package of programs to ensure skill development in school, remedial skill-building for out-of-school young people, and retraining for adults as well. Keenly aware of the challenge presented by the 1992 integration of the Common Market, the British realize that competitiveness will be judged on product quality and that product quality will be determined by worker quality.

Despite their deep-seated cultural and political differences, all three countries can read the writing on the economic wall.

In addition to these and other individual workforce competence-building programs, there are at least three EEC-wide action programs currently under way: (1) a program to smooth the transition of young people from school to work with a special emphasis on industry partnerships; (2) a program to raise the standards of post-compulsory school vocational training to ensure that it results in recognized qualifications; and (3) a parallel program to upgrade and keep current the working-world relevance of compulsory school curricula. Thus, even as they compete with each other, EEC countries are also cooperating with each other on the workforce competence issue, even to the extent of establishing a special fund to provide technical assistance to lesser-developed members such as Spain, Portugal, Greece, and Ireland.

I've written a book, called *SchoolWorks*, for the German Marshall Fund of the United States exploring some of these workforce education and training programs in detail. In this article, let me present just a few basic principles I draw from the successes in Europe:

Principle 1. Work is the defining element of human existence; cash income maintenance payments do not substitute for work. European education and skill development systems are aimed at assuring the currency and marketability of the skills of every single adult, not just those who are unemployed. But they also take pains to move those who *have* been shunted aside, for whatever reason, back into the mainstream. The priorities are as follows: (1) make sure basic needs are met, (2) provide education or training immediately, (3) provide a clear path to a job and placement assistance, and then and only then (4) provide welfare payments for those who cannot secure work, but make them contingent upon continued participation in training and employment efforts. Investments are significant, but felt to be far less than the cost of widespread welfare and associated social pathologies.

Principle 2. The key to producing a work-ready workforce is a first-rate educational system with an explicit and significant work experience component. In the absence of connections with the world of work, education flirts with irrelevance. In addition to assuring that young people leave school with recognized credentials, the connection to the world of work also helps the educational system to adapt to change in the real world, keeping it fresh and current. How European nations make the connection between school and work varies with their experience and cultural traditions, but the commitment to a seamless transition from school to work is absolute.

Principle 3. Public education and job-training programs must provide their clients with recognized and accepted credentials. The 1992 integration of markets for products and services has forced European countries to implement what in the U.S. is still a theoretical notion: that people should have "portable skills"—that is, that their credentials should be universally recognized and respected. The competition created by 1992 demands such a system. In the U.S., competition—from Europe, the Far East, and elsewhere—is not yet immediate enough to force this issue, yet it is just as real. We know that recognized quality is what creates competitiveness; we must understand that recognized workforce skill is what creates quality. Since we can no longer survive simply by trading with ourselves, we must respond to this principle.

Principle 4. Creating a competitive workforce requires partnerships between labor, business, and government.   Not even the most centralized European nation pretends that creating a highly skilled workforce can be accomplished by government alone. In one form or another all of these programs are jointly conceived and executed by labor, business, and government, and the role of business owners is crucial—both in the development of policy and in its operation.

Principle 5. There are no quick fixes; building workforce competence requires long-term investments and a patient, experimental attitude.   Especially in Sweden, but elsewhere as well, establishing first-rate education and training systems has involved steady and patient planning, trying, evaluating, revising, and trying again—recognizing that no one has "the answer" and that, in any event, the target is constantly moving. What's more, the best programs are customer driven and must change as customer needs change. The best programs require a commitment and investment by participants and, in turn, must assure participants that they will have the flexibility to craft their own futures. In contrast, U.S. programs are forever in search of the single sweeping solution and typically force clients to jump through eligibility hoops that have little to do with their real needs or interests. As a consequence, they fail—expensively.

Principle 6. Compulsory school cannot produce fully prepared workers; everyone needs further training.   Even Europe's best, most working-world–relevant compulsory school systems—and they are very, very good—don't expect their graduates to be fully prepared for the world of work. In every case, some post-compulsory school training system is in place—both for students entering the workforce, and for workers who wish to, or must, change jobs. Where the concept of "life-long learning" is a trendy bit of theory among education professionals in the U.S., it is an accepted fact of life for individuals in many European countries and in the businesses for which they work.

In the end, the European and American approaches to economic competitiveness boil down to a simple distinction: While the United States worries about the competitiveness of companies, many European nations focus on the competitiveness of *individuals*, believing—I think correctly—that when individuals are competitive, companies and nations will be competitive as well.

Technology Development: Perspectives on the Third Wave

———————————————— Walter H. Plosila

Technology innovation and development emerged as a major component of state and local economic development strategies during the 1980s. By the end of the decade, forty-four states had some type of technology program.

These state programs could be classified in several ways. The predominant program component was technology and research centers—accounting for 41 percent of state technology development funds—followed by research and development grants, technology transfer mechanisms, seed/venture capital funds, and technical and managerial assistance. In addition, many states and localities initiated major capital programs for research center facilities and equipment, set up incubators, and launched research parks.

By and large, most state and local efforts were designed to intervene at a later stage in the innovation process than had traditionally been characteristic of the federal science and technology policy, focused largely on basic research, that preceded them. A few states—Michigan and Pennsylvania, for example—began to provide services throughout the innovation process.

The 1980s boon: New emphases

As would be expected in a period of ferment and experimentation, many of these relatively new state and local efforts were fragmented, haphazardly organized, and not well-linked to—or reinforcing of—each other. On the other hand, the programs offered the paradigm of state and local economic development practice several new emphases, namely:

Reprinted by permission of the Corporation For Enterprise Development (CFED) from *Entrepreneurial Economy Review* (Autumn 1990): 11–15. CFED, 777 North Capitol St., N.E., #801, Washington, D. C. 20002.

Risk: a new interest in risk-oriented programs, including equity, seed, venture and working capital investments

Credibility: a recognition that technology is an important component of assistance to traditional industries, particularly manufacturing

Higher education: an increased awareness that higher educational institutions play a crucial role in state and local economic development

Entrepreneurs: an increased interest in working with and involving entrepreneur-driven businesses; this was in contrast to public agency focus on Fortune 500 firms during the 1960s and 1970s.

As to the effectiveness of individual components of these 1980s-style technology innovation efforts, the jury is still out. It may stay out for a considerable while, due to the failure to build accountability and assessment measures into these programs from the outset.

At the same time, evidence is emerging from programs like Pennsylvania's Ben Franklin Partnership, Ohio's Thomas Edison Technology Centers and Indiana's Corporation for Science and Technology that new relationships have been forged and new capacities established that link technology to economic development. Moreover, at least a few jurisdictions are establishing new public sector roles and functions.

Models for impact

State and local technology development programs, like other components of economic development strategy, need new organizational structures, new types of delivery systems and modes of operation, and improved management and development incentives. In short, they need to adopt Third Wave principles.

Third Wave thinking has already arrived in some aspects of state and local technology development effort. But more is called for. Five aspects of the design of state and local technology development efforts should be addressed: leverage, operating intermediaries, competitive and incentive-driven framework, integrating efforts, and accountability.

Leverage   Several technology development programs adhere to one Third Wave principle: they require that private sector funding be committed to the effort before public resource commitments are made. But more need to follow this leveraging principle.

One example is Pennsylvania's Ben Franklin Partnership Program, which links private sector firms with the specific research capabilities of educational institutions to help "spin-in" advanced technology applications to existing industries and "spin-off" new products and firms on the leading edge of innovation. The Partnership's grant program requires that one dollar of private support

The Edison Welding Institute: An intermediary organization

The Edison Welding Institute is a functioning example of a Third Wave intermediary organization for technology development. Located in Columbus, Ohio, the Edison Welding Institute (EWI) is one of Ohio's nine Edison Technology Centers. The Institute represents the type of intermediary organization that brokers and utilizes the resources of government, industry and higher education through shared ownership. To date, it has received over $30 million in state, industrial and university support.

EWI was formed out of the merger of a National Science Foundation–funded university-based center, the welding activities of a contract research center—Battelle Memorial Institute—and the U.S. members of the United Kingdom–based Welding Institute.

Today, EWI works closely with Ohio State University's Welding Engineering Department, particularly in basic research areas that take best advantage of faculty interests and expertise. Ohio State, as part owner of EWI, has provided five years of rent-free use of one of its buildings, and holds two seats on the Board of Trustees.

EWI is operated by its 228 industrial members, who elect its Board of Trustees as well as an Industrial Advisory Board. The Board selects research projects and establishes service priorities.

The Institute is organized into three units—research, education and applications.

Research   Research may be cooperative, involving Ohio State University and one or more members as well as EWI staff; it may be a single-firm project or a group project. Confidential proprietary research activities are permitted and members have a say over how their dues are divided between core efforts, specific services, and research projects they wish to sponsor.

Education   The education and training agenda of EWI builds on the results of its research efforts, integrating the results of research into education and training services. Educational activities include opportunities for member firms to interact with EWI's 50-person staff, and to participate in workshops, seminars and conferences. EWI provides a considerable amount of information to its members through videotapes, inspection and training aids, and training and development consulting services. The education and training role includes "hands-on" work—even designing operator and maintenance manuals and providing customized training programs for large and small member firms.

Applications   The third major focus of EWI—applications—also builds on the Institute's research expertise, actively assisting firms to use research in their operations. EWI's applications work can include providing problem-solving services to one or more members at a firm's site or at EWI's facilities. Applications engineering services assure that the Institute not only "thinks" but "acts" to improve the manufacturing competitiveness of its members.

match each dollar of public support. The university and the firm involved in a project with the Center must reach agreement—and put their commitment in writing—before public funds are released. Likewise, before an Ohio Thomas Edison Technology Center can expend public funds, the private sector match must be in hand. Such leverage provisions and private sector commitments allow the market to drive the program, helping to assure that the private sector is setting the agenda.

Another example of leveraging is found in several states' efforts to increase the seed and venture capital available to start-up firms. Replacing the traditional loan finance programs directly operated by government, seed/venture efforts in Pennsylvania, Michigan and Maryland have attempted to leverage public funds and, in the process, permanently change private sector behavior. These states have required between a 2- and 3-to-1 private-to-public ratio for the dollars a client firm raises.

Moreover, some states invest public funds to create larger, privately-managed funds. The public role, besides being lead investor, is limited to selection of the general manager and certification of the match, along with after-the-fact monitoring of results. Public funds are treated in these deals much like private funds—as investments that carry both the risk of failure and the possibility for good return. The public policy objective? Stimulate greater amounts of private funds for firms at the critical start-up and expansion stages, but do so in a way that will encourage a long-term change in private sector behavior and practice—that is, more ongoing investment in seed and expansion capital.

Operating intermediaries Effective state technology development programs, rather than take on day-to-day program management and functional responsibilities themselves, have operated through locally-owned intermediaries, usually non-profit organizations. In contrast to most public bureaucracies, these intermediaries are able to respond quickly to industry's demands. They are flexible in attitude, responsive to the customer, and see their role as investors—all aspects of Third Wave organizations. They function as what Richard Hatch calls "brokers," or facilitators, rather than as direct service providers.

Although they seem to have some characteristics of intermediaries, university technology centers, whether based on campus or in an affiliate arrangement, are by and large still making Second Wave adjustments. Many states, including New York, New Jersey, Minnesota, Kansas, Iowa, Maryland, Virginia, Washington, and Utah, have used such centers. But the firms they serve have generally been Fortune 500, not the newly important small- and medium-sized firms. Their focus has been the development of basic or fundamental knowledge, with only minimal attention devoted to critical services like technology transfer, testbeds, demonstrations, market information and applied R&D.

But there are now many examples of movement toward using effective intermediaries. High Technology Councils have been established throughout the U.S.—in Pittsburgh, Kansas City, Chicago, suburban Maryland—to be network brokers. Effective, technology-oriented incubators in some communities have gone beyond simply serving their tenants, playing a broader broker role in their communities. Some state technology development programs locate primary decisionmaking responsibility in regional broker organizations. Intermediaries don't always do it all themselves; they often contract out for R&D and other entrepreneurial development functions, the Ben Franklin Centers being a good example. State and local government roles in these entities range from partial owner or investor to promoter.

Other new organization models are emerging that provide an additional alternative to the traditional research centers. These mechanisms, generally called "consortia" or "networks," are more often found in Europe than the U.S., and are designed to service small and medium-sized firms. In my parlance, both consortia and networks are groups of firms that come together to define, organize and/or provide some needed information or technical assistance service. Consortia are more formally established, with staff and facilities, whereas networks may involve less formal associations among firms, without dedicated staff. In either case, they are "market driven" in design and implementation, with a particular focus on product prototype design, technology transfer and international marketing services.

Three standout U.S. examples of consortia include Ohio's Edison Technology Centers, the Michigan Strategic Fund–supported Technology Centers, and Pennsylvania's Ben Franklin Partnership Programs, supplemented by a new initiative to form networks through trade associations. These new structures include some of the key components of a Third Wave organizational design for technology development:

Centers are non-profit membership organizations, private and independent, with shared involvement by industry, university and government partners.

Higher education is an important but not dominant partner.

The public sector role is primarily limited to that of catalyst or facilitator.

Public support is given for both core (research) and proprietary (product development) projects using a competitive process.

Public funds leverage private funds with private sector commitments made up-front.

Centers provide a comprehensive range of services, with particular emphasis on design, marketing and information services. R&D is not the exclusive focus.

Competitive and incentive-driven framework   Ohio and Pennsylvania have built another Third Wave principle—competition—into their technology development efforts. In each case, state-supported centers compete for a share of state funds available. They must demonstrate, both on a quantitative and qualitative basis, that they meet overall program objectives.

Another example of incentive-driven effort is technology incubators, usually located near universities. In return for access to university resources and below–market-rate rents, incubator tenants at the University of Maryland and Lehigh University must give up a small equity in their firm. Public funds help underwrite the incubator's operations. In turn, locating in an incubator helps improve a firm's survival rate, securing the public's long-term investment in the firm.

Integrating efforts   Technology development efforts embrace many state or local government agencies and departments. But technology programs have generally failed to establish synergy among these agencies. In part, this has been due to a lack of an overall set of policies and strategies to provide a common framework under which reinforcement and linkages might occur.

Intermediary organizations can play a critical role linking action, policy and strategy, serving as sort of a "railroad roundhouse," directing traffic, resources, and activities. Pennsylvania's Ben Franklin Partnership Centers do this, with over $25 million in annual project grants to use as an incentive, along with a mandate to do much more than R&D. New York and Maryland have set up regional councils that play a similar role, but without benefit of grant funds to administer.

Assigning delivery of programs to the regional and local levels, rewarding performance and linkages through a competitive allocation process, and sending the same message of reinforcement to each element of the delivery system will more reasonably assure that efforts will be integrated than will any coordination by government fiat.

Accountability   Because public technology development programs have generally lacked a competitive nature, they have also discouraged the development of accountability mechanisms. In the new efforts, one surrogate accountability mechanism is the leveraging of private sector funds. Private sector funds and support are not likely to continue over multiple years if progress—and profits—are not being achieved. In short, leveraging is a good design measure for accountability as well as impact.

Unfortunately, nearly half the state and local technology investment in this country still goes to research centers, many of which do not require matching funds or industrial involvement in their efforts. Consortia and networks, on the other hand, are by design required to establish accountability. Their members will not renew or pay their dues if they are not satisfied. Consortia, while having to expend considerable time in maintaining membership satisfaction, provide a market-driven alternative to research centers. Consortia services—like transferring technology and providing market and design services—generate direct member feedback, assuring more effective utilization of resources.

Eight design rules for impact

State and local technology development efforts represent "novel experiments" and are important components in building state and local entrepreneurial economies. Small firms account for much of the innovation in this country and a disproportionate share of the job growth. Large firms rely on technological innovations from small firms to maintain their competitive edge. If state and local technology development efforts are to contribute to these efforts at a sufficient scale and with significant impact, they must give more attention to Third Wave organization and design characteristics. Utilizing Third Wave principles, I can suggest eight rules for improving the design and operation of state and local technology innovation programs in the 1990s.

Build networks and consortia. Give as much, if not more, support to building network and consortia arrangements as is now given to university-based research and industrial affiliate centers.

Establish local intermediaries. Develop local intermediary organizations with sufficient flexibility and resources to offer incentives for linked programs and efforts.

Wholesale services and programs. Provide funds and services on a "wholesale" basis to such intermediaries, allowing them to leverage those resources and become the service delivery agent for their natural constituencies, instead of having state government itself directly provide—or "retail"—its programs. This helps build local ownership and private sector leadership.

Require leverage and commitment. Assure a more market-driven approach by building such principles as leverage and private sector commitment into public policies and decisions.

Make policies and programs comprehensive. Address technological innovation through comprehensive rather than narrowly-defined programs. For example, don't separate the needs of manufacturers from the rest of industry, or limit a program to simply funding R&D while not including an entrepreneurial support role.

Generate competition. Provide ongoing funding through a competitive process. It designs accountability *in* and furnishes a basis for future investment.

Fill gaps and change behavior. Design and provide public programs that fill actual gaps in needed activity and encourage changes in private sector behavior—so that the gaps don't reappear in the future.

Invest, don't grant. Use public funds as investments rather than as grants or loans to firms. This compels both the public and private sectors to share risk and reward.

State and local technology development efforts should remain pluralistic. There are roles for higher education institutions and research centers, matching grants, incubators, and seed and venture capital. Third Wave principles can help guide and improve these programs, further demonstrating the effectiveness of these experiments in our states, regions and communities.

A Poverty Program
That Works

David Osborne

Picture a black urban community of 80,000 in which crime, drug abuse, and unemployment have reached such levels that landlords are deserting their buildings rather than trying to sell them. Now picture the same neighborhood 15 years later, with $160 million in new investments, 350 large apartment buildings rehabilitated, and property values rising five to seven percent a year. Hundreds of businesses have started, and thousands of people have received remedial education, job training, and job placement. The community is stable, crime is down, and the crack epidemic hasn't taken root. Yet none of this has been accomplished through gentrification. The community is still 99 percent black. Rents are still fairly low. People on welfare can still afford to move in.

Now imagine that all this is the result of an anti-poverty program that cost only $10 million to $12 million. If this were a government program, we would have replicated it a thousand times and declared victory in the war on poverty. But it isn't, so we have virtually ignored it.

The "program" is the Shorebank Corporation, in Chicago's South Shore neighborhood. Shorebank is a holding company that includes a bank, a real estate development corporation, a small venture capital firm, and something called The Neighborhood Institute, which does low-income housing development, remedial education, vocational training, and the like. Within a small circle of foundation people and anti-poverty activists, Shorebank is legendary. In Washington it is almost unknown. Yet it is the perfect model for the 1990s: inexpensive, market-oriented, and entrepreneurial.

Because it is subsidized by philanthropists, Shorebank does something the private sector normally cannot do: it makes investments whose returns are often slim to nonexistent. Because it is a business that will go under if it makes too many bad investments, it does something government normally cannot do: it invests only in people who have the savvy and commitment to succeed, whether by starting a business, acquiring a skill and a job, or buying and renovating an apartment building. Government normally spends its money in response to community desires, political clout, or need. Shorebank seeks out those who can thrive in the marketplace, then gives them support. In the long run, success in the marketplace—not good intentions or piles of money—is what improves people's lives.

Shorebank's one big weakness is that although it pays for itself, it is not profitable enough to convince other entrepreneurs with capital to imitate its success. After 15 years, it is clear that the Shorebank model will not spread unless the public sector is willing to invest.

Shorebank was the brainchild of Ron Grzywinski, a graying 53-year-old who looks and talks more like a scholar than an entrepreneur. In the late 1960s Grzywinski owned a small bank in Hyde Park, home of the University of Chicago. Adlai Stevenson III was state treasurer. Searching for a way to help the ghettos, Stevenson decided to deposit state funds only in banks that agreed to create units specializing in minority business lending. Grzywinski asked Milton Davis, a former Chicago chairman of the Congress on Racial Equality (CORE), to run his minority business program. "We were getting tired of sitting in and getting thrown out by the Chicago police, and we were discussing what else we could do," Davis remembers. "But I must confess it had never occurred to me that a bank might be a vehicle."

Davis hired Jim Fletcher, a black assistant director in the federal Community Action Program—who, like Davis, had no experience in banking. Grzywinski hired Mary Houghton, a white 27-year-old graduate of the Johns Hopkins School of Advanced International Studies. Together, the four of them made the program work. "Because we were running something that was less torpid and more serious than the large banks were, we outperformed them," says Houghton. "And we just got to thinking, 'Well, if we can do this trick, what would be the next trick?'"

Chicago is often considered the most segregated city in America. Residents joke that the definition of integration is the period between the arrival of the first black family and the departure of the last white family. When neighborhoods go from white to black, banks and other institutions normally quit investing, hastening the slide into decay and depopulation. Watching this happen all around Hyde Park, Grzywinski and company began talking about how to reverse the process, how to bring capital back into black communities. Gradually the idea of using a bank as the stable, profit-making base for other development efforts emerged. Grzywinski wrote an offering circular that, in his words, "said we were trying to raise $4 million in common stock, in units of $160,000 each, to purchase an unknown bank in an unknown neighborhood, to test an untested idea."

When South Shore Bank came on the market, Grzywinski had raised only $800,000. But the opportunity was too good to resist. Only a few miles south of Hyde Park, the South Shore neighborhood was not yet too far gone to help. As a white community, it had been middle and upper-middle class, with single-family homes of all sizes and gracious, red brick apartment buildings from the 1920s. It was bordered by Lake Michigan on the west and a park on the north and was only 15 minutes from downtown Chicago. Despite a 98 percent racial turnover in the preceding decade, the neighborhood was still perhaps two-thirds middle and working class, only one-third underclass.

For all its amenities, however, South Shore was headed rapidly downhill. "There were no loans being made," says James Lowell, community affairs manager for the Federal Reserve Board. "The bank wanted to pull out; it did not want to deal with black people, period. The neighborhood was going to lose its park, because the city felt it was just going to be a crime hazard. The shoreline was becoming a disaster area. A lot of those old, beautiful buildings were just crumbling. An awful lot of units had been walked away from."

Dorris Pickens, the president of Shorebank's Neighborhood Institute, has lived in South Shore since 1970. She and her husband—then a lineman for the Chicago Bears—were among the thousands of blacks who moved to South Shore because it was an attractive neighborhood, only to see the bottom drop out. "When we moved in," she says, "I bet 70 percent of the people on our block were white. And they just left. They didn't say goodbye, they just disappeared. It was like they moved out at night."

In 1973 Grzywinski and his colleagues bought the bank, putting down their $800,000 and borrowing the rest—more than $2.4 million. They launched a variety of aggressive lending programs: single-family mortgages, small-business loans, consumer loans. The mortgage lending worked. Though not one other bank or savings and loan would lend in the neighborhood—bankers had reflexively begun redlining as soon as the neighborhood went black—Shorebank had no problem with foreclosures, and by 1980 other institutions had entered the market.

Most of Shorebank's other efforts failed, however. Between 1974 and 1980 Grzywinski and his colleagues loaned $6.7 million and provided heavy technical support to small businesses. Outside of loans to McDonald's franchises, the results were dismal. Most of the businesses went under, and by 1980, 71st Street, the main shopping strip, looked worse than it had in 1973. With small stores and little parking—not to mention threatening teenagers loitering on the sidewalks—71st Street merchants could not compete with the shopping malls. The most dramatic failure came when a black merchant located catercorner from the bank—who was one of Shorebank's first and most promising borrowers—tied up two Small Business Administration employees who had come to foreclose on him and burned down his building, with them inside.

Throughout the '70s the bank limped along, its profits in the bottom 25 percent of all banks, federal examiners pressuring its managers to tighten up their loan portfolios. As high interest rates buffeted the Rustbelt economy, two black-owned banks on the edge of the neighborhood failed. South Shore Bank survived primarily through the invention of what it called "development deposits": large deposits made by institutions and wealthy individuals who shared the bank's social goals. Some depositors accept below-market rates to subsidize Shorebank's work, but generally these deposits offer market rates of interest. Even so, it took an intensive nationwide effort to attract them, since the bank's neighborhood wasn't exactly filled with eager depositors. Today development deposits account for almost half of the bank's $150 million deposit base.

Gradually it became clear that the key to stabilizing the neighborhood wasn't so much reviving its commercial areas as rehabilitating the apartment buildings that housed 70 percent of its people. When buildings are abandoned in a neighborhood like South Shore—as they were in rising numbers throughout the '70s—the empty hulks become targets for arson, hangouts for drug dealers, and homes for junkies. Crime grows, law-abiding residents flee, and more buildings are abandoned. Once things get that bad, no amount of loans or rehab projects will stop the process. Besides, most residents worked outside of South Shore, so bringing jobs in was less important to them than saving the existing housing. Milton Davis recalls: "They were saying, what are you going to do with upgraded commercial areas if you have nobody living in the neighborhood?"

At the time, financial institutions refused to offer mortgages on apartment buildings in Chicago's poor, black neighborhoods. They had tried and—as Grzywinski was warned by the chairman of one local savings and loan—they had failed. But Shorebank's managers decided to try anyway. They put in charge a young man who had started with the bank as a teller supervisor, Jim Bringley. Bringley is a nuts-and-bolts, blue-collar, get-it-done type. Slowly, carefully, he began lending to people who wanted to buy apartment buildings. He started with three- and six-flat buildings and gradually moved up. He only made loans in South Shore, and only to people who agreed to rehab their buildings. He then worked with them closely, even sponsoring monthly meetings where the growing stable of landlords could swap trade secrets.

For the most part, they were people who had never before been landlords. "Real estate here doesn't make sense for investors. It's gotta be for hands-on people," Bringley says. "It's generally people with blue-collar mentalities, who don't mind spending nights and weekends. It's not a coat-and-tie business—the dirtier you come in the better. . . . You go in and buy a bad building, you got drug dealers, you gotta get these people out."

As the new landlords filled up one building with paying tenants, they bought another, then another. Today South Shore has a core of about 50 housing entrepreneurs, some of whom own as many as ten buildings. They have learned the trade; some have taught themselves Spanish to communicate with their low-cost crews. By investing in the neighborhood's primary resource, its housing stock, they have kicked off a development process that has its own momentum; each renovated apartment building adds to the value of the last, and makes the next one easier.

Driving South Shore's tree-lined streets, one sees elegant courtyard buildings that would fit well into the tonier north side neighborhoods. The brick is freshly sandblasted; the grounds are immaculate; wrought-iron fences and gates lend the old buildings an air of grace. There are still pockets of decay, but the better blocks bring to mind a white, well-to-do community in the 1940s, not a black, inner-city neighborhood in the 1980s.

As important as Bringley's entrepreneurs have been to South Shore, there are some areas they would not touch. One area, known as Parkside, had been designated the site of an urban renewal project that was never carried through. With seizure by eminent domain seemingly a certainty, landlords had quit maintaining their buildings. By the mid-'70s, nearly half of the large apartment buildings in the area were tax delinquent, most on their way to abandonment.

After taking a close look, Bringley concluded that no rational person would buy and rehab a building there. He recommended a large, government-subsidized rehab project as the only way to stem the area's decline. City Lands Corporation, Shorebank's real estate development firm, brought in First National Bank of Chicago and another real estate development firm as partners, and together they structured a package that used heavy public subsidies and syndication to limited partners, who invested as a tax shelter. They bought 25 buildings, tore down five for parking lots, and ended up with 446 units of moderate- and low-income housing—the largest such rehab project in state history. With deep federal subsidies, they did not have to skimp. And Shorebank's managers screened applicants carefully with an eye to minimizing drug and crime problems. Parkways, as the project was dubbed, now looks more like an expensive condominium complex than a low-income housing project.

Elsewhere in South Shore, City Lands has rehabbed another 480 units. It will soon break ground on an eight-acre shopping center on 71st Street, which will provide the large stores and parking necessary to compete with the malls. The Neighborhood Institute (TNI) has rehabbed another 275 units, while offering remedial education and job training for people who are on welfare or unemployed. It runs a small business incubator, which gives inexpensive space and intensive management assistance to small businesses, and it plans two other incubators in the neighborhood. Finally, it provides training for entrepreneurs—including welfare mothers—who run or want to run their own businesses.

It is harder to gauge the effectiveness of TNI's training and business development efforts than that of Shorebank's housing work, because trained employees are far less visible than renovated buildings. But TNI has placed more than 2,700 of its trainees in jobs, counseled more than 1,000 entrepreneurs, and assisted roughly 70 start-up firms. Though it depends more heavily on public money than do the other Shorebank companies (because it is trying to help the neighborhood's poorest people), it is still forced to search for people who are capable of succeeding in the marketplace. Its training contracts with the city and state are performance based, meaning it doesn't get paid until it has successfully placed a trainee in a job. And its incubator will fail unless it stays relatively full of businesses that pay their rent. Overall, TNI earns about 90 percent of its $1.7 million operating budget—from training contracts, fees earned in developing and managing buildings, and rents.

Financially, 1988 was Shorebank's best year ever. In a neighborhood where 70 percent of loan recipients (through 1980) had never before borrowed from a financial institution, the bank earned a $1.7 million profit—about average for a bank of its size. Virtually no real estate loans went bad, and even the commercial loans performed well.

As a community, South Shore not only has stabilized, it is improving markedly. The people who have bought and renovated apartment buildings serve as gatekeepers to the community, evicting drug users and criminals. Crime is way down, and the black middle class is staying. Under pressure from the community, the police have finally cleared out the El Rukns gang (descendants of the old Blackstone Rangers), whose presence kept one corner of the neighborhood from blossoming. The gang's headquarters building is being demolished, and TNI hopes to do a massive, Parkways-style development in the area.

South Shore is doing so well that Shorebank has targeted a second Chicago neighborhood, Austin. City Lands and TNI have 600 units of housing rehabilitation under way there, and Shorebank's entry has touched off a small speculative boom, encouraging other developers to begin work on another 1,400 units. Shorebank has convinced the Illinois Housing Authority, a prestigious business group called Chicago United, and the Federal National Mortgage

Association to target Austin. The Housing Authority provides rehab subsidies, Chicago United will focus primarily on job training and education, and FNMA will provide $5 million for low–down payment mortgages.

Shorebank's managers do not claim that their model would work in the very worst ghettos. But the worst ghettos, which get the most attention, are actually less representative of the typical poor neighborhood than are South Shore and Austin. (Actually, Shorebank's success may make the worst ghettos worse. The drug dealers and pimps who are cleared out by South Shore's landlords have to go somewhere, so South Shore's gain is some poorer neighborhood's loss. This is unfortunate, but if we are to rescue any of urban black America, it is probably inevitable. The culture of crime, drug abuse, and poverty can engulf community after community if we let it. The first step toward eliminating it is to confine it—to secure at least some inner-city neighborhoods where black children can grow up with role models who make a good living doing honest work.)

For most poor neighborhoods, Shorebank's success offers great hope and teaches important lessons. First, it demonstrates the necessity of changing the marketplace in a poor community, rather than simply spending more money. In many poor communities, the only inflow of capital is government transfer payments. In South Shore, money is coming in for *investment*, which means that it is being steered toward productive people, and therefore is likely to generate more money.

Second, Shorebank demonstrates the psychological power of a bank. Unlike government programs, banks inspire confidence. They have the credibility needed to convince other financial institutions to invest. And they send an unmistakable signal to a community's residents: people with money have confidence in the future of this neighborhood. Also, residents view a bank not as a program designed to do something for them, but as a source of credit they can use to do something for themselves. If the government can be convinced to subsidize programs like Shorebank, keeping them free from the government's taint will be a critical challenge.

Third, Shorebank demonstrates the importance of scale. Few poverty programs are of sufficient size to make more than a dent. South Shore Bank has invested more than $107 million since 1973, while TNI and City Lands have brought in another $65 million. Together, the three have financed more than 7,000 housing units. (These figures include Austin.)

Finally, Shorebank demonstrates the power of combining the investment methods of the private sector with the social goals of the public sector. The subsidy provided by Shorebank's equity investors has allowed it to invest where normal banks could not. But Shorebank is still at risk in the marketplace; to survive it must make investments that result in successful individuals, businesses, or buildings. If it doesn't—if Grzywinski and his colleagues don't get some return on their investments—they'll soon be unemployed (and, more important in their particular case, they'll have seen their dream die).

Shorebank is creating a slightly different version of the model in rural Arkansas, in partnership with the Winthrop Rockefeller Foundation. Others are trying to replicate the Chicago model in New York, Washington, and Omaha. But none of the three has been able to raise the $5 million to $10 million they need to get started. This is where government must step in. If we want to see more Shorebanks, we need a source of capital. (We also need an institute to train the people who will run them, but that's another story.) Without government as an investor, the most dramatic inner-city success story of our time will remain the exception, not the rule.

This is not to say the model will be easy to copy, even with government help. Shorebank's success depends, to an unknown degree, on the extraordinary qualities of the people who run it. Moreover, an important part of that success lies in the program's very insulation from the deadening hand of government bureaucracy. If government is willing to provide equity investments to private development banks (and, perhaps, access to government deposits, favorable interest rates from the Fed, and so on) but not to demand more control than any other equity investor, a development bank program might work. If government treats development banks as *government programs*, required to meet all the public accountability standards and to jump through all the bureaucratic hoops, it will never work.

"Sometime in the last century or before," Grzywinski says, "we figured out ways to create universities and hospitals as major not-for-profit organizations that were capitalized either with public funds or private funds, to achieve a public purpose. We created them in a way that they would be substantial, permanent, and in the marketplace. They have to be managed like businesses. And one could ask, 'Why don't we create development institutions the same way?'"

PART 3

The New Economic Geography

The Suburban Growth Corridor: Defining the New Economic Geometry

George Sternlieb and James W. Hughes

The enormous U.S. commercial construction boom/bust of the 1980s has been a staple of the mass media. Tales are commonplace of real estate fortunes giving way to record vacancy levels in the mineral and natural resource capitals of Houston or Denver. At the other end of the spectrum has been a shift in attention from New York's demise to the phenomena of Madison Avenue store rents of $300 per square foot and White Plains traffic gridlock. And it is the latter that has elicited the new media fascination: the suburban growth corridor. A Princeton corridor in New Jersey, with more than 10 million square feet of office space—little of it more than a few years old—has many counterparts throughout the country.

What has not been appreciated, however, is that the sheer scale of this construction binge has defined the pattern of suburban/exurban development for the next decade. Aided and abetted by generous—perhaps overgenerous—tax depreciation allowances, the future skeleton of the American economy is being set in concrete. While many suburban growth zones may be currently overbuilt, the very scale of development that has been occurring within these zones serves to limit the potential of alternative future sites—both center city and exurban.

The development community took nearly a generation to

Reprinted with permission from *Economic Development Commentary* (Spring 1986). *Economic Development Commentary* is published quarterly by the National Council for Urban Economic Development. CUED is recognized as the preeminent national organization serving local development professionals from both the public and private sectors. Throughout the year, CUED supports its members through timely conferences, up-to-date information, legislative reports and newsletters, thorough review of specific economic development techniques in its quarterly journal, and access to some of the best economic development reports in the country.

awaken fully to the possibilities of the new 100 percent locations—
the metropolitan circumferential highways and their radial corridor
outgrowths. It has taken only a half-dozen years to build well past
the market saturation level. The "bargain" rents spawned by the
current speculative boom, however, will slow future growth. The
ongoing joke in the Houston market is five years' free rent for a
three-year lease! As this scenario multiples, the ramifications will
be substantial, but a suburbanized economy will have come of age
and with it new public policy implications.

Development or debacle?

The very name "suburb" still conjures up visions of an earlier era—
quaint bedroom hamlets populated by downtown commuters. But
today, large-scale post-industrial corporate settlements and their
service retinues define the development action. A new shape and
logic prevail. The basic numbers on office construction and its location tell the tale.

The arithmetic of the sizzling 1980s' office market and the di-
lemma of overexpansion are relatively straightforward. As detailed
in the *1986 Dodge/Sweet's Construction Outlook*, from 1981 through
1985, the U.S. economy was able to digest about 250 million square
feet of new office construction per year. But during this five-year
period, annual additions to the office inventory averaged 300 million
square feet. As residential construction faltered from the record
years of the 1970s, the nation's builders went on an office construction binge. Over 1.5 billion square feet of office space were constructed between 1981 and 1985, a quantity sufficient to shelter the
entire service-producing sector of the West German economy.

But the gap between space availability and the U.S. economy's
consumption requirements is growing, suggesting that substantial
cutbacks are going to be required in the level of new construction to
absorb the present and pending overhang. The future is clear and is
based on the following rationale.

Office space allocated per office worker has expanded enormously over time. Planners were using a parameter of approximately 150 square feet per worker as late as the mid-1960s; the present standard is slightly in excess of 200 square feet. The reasons
for this growth vary, from the necessity of housing more equipment
per worker associated with office automation to the tendency for
firms to rent not the space they currently need—but the square
footage they envision growing into. Considering current space requirements in conjunction with employment projections (in excess
of 1 million office jobs per year) and estimates of obsolete building
replacement, *Dodge/Sweet's Construction Outlook* projects a sustain-
able future demand of 250 million square feet for the balance of this
decade. This is consistent with the actual experience of the first half
of the 1980s.

With an excess over normal vacancy rates of between 200 and

250 million square feet of space already available to meet this demand, only 200 million square feet of new construction per year can be justified for the next five years. This is fully one-third less than the preceding five years (1981–1985), but it still may represent an optimistic expectation.

While there has been much discussion of wholesale obsolescence of older office facilities as "smart" structures are required to house modern electronic equipment, this rationale has not yet provided sufficient justification for increased utilization of newer buildings at the cost of the old. Indeed, an argument can be made that 1980s' electronics require less in the way of building retrofitting, heavy-duty air conditioning, etc., than did the predecessor technologies of a decade ago. And as paper storage of records gives way to enormously capacious electronic memories, the potential of physical shrinkage is made even more evident.

There are striking flywheels of custom that inhibit change, as witness the law firm library continuing to occupy expensive space while the researchers use LEXIS, a legal data base. But finally even this is made mutable by time, thus potentially reducing ultimate space requirements.

Increasing suburban dominance

Somewhere in the mid-1970s, for the first time in history, more office space was projected for suburbia than for the classic central business district (CBD). While this was not achieved until after the decade ended, the scale of suburban dominance of this traditional, central-city downtown function is remarkable. By 1985, two out of every three square feet of new office construction was begun in suburbia.

The vigor of change is indicated in Table 1, which illustrates

Table 1. 1985 office space in 24 metropolitan areas (million square feet).
Source: The Office Network Inc., National Office Market Report, Fall/Winter, 1985.

Total existing office space	Number	Percent	Existing space available	Number	Percent
Total	1,333.2	100.0	Total	217.5	100.0
CBD	580.3	43.5	CBD	75.7	34.8
Suburban	752.9	56.5	Suburban	141.8	65.2
Total under construction			Under construction (available for lease)		
Total	177.1	100.0	Total	148.4	100.0
CBD	64.6	36.5	CBD	52.1	35.1
Suburban	112.5	63.5	Suburban	96.3	64.9

Note: In 1981, the suburban market (outside CBD) accounted for only 48.6 percent of existing office space.

office space in 24 major metropolitan areas in 1985 as compiled by
The Office Network. In the areas under consideration, there was a
total of 1.3 billion square feet of existing office space. Only 43.5 percent of it, however, was in the CBD; the balance was in suburbia,
compared to only 48.6 percent in suburbia in 1981. The dispropor-
tion is made even more evident when the total space under construction is isolated: 63.5 percent is suburban.

The sheer vigor of suburbanization has yielded even greater
shares of the space available (vacancies), as contrasted with the central business district. The very fact that funding can be secured—
and buildings generated—in the face of such vacancy concentrations
indicates not only the problems of a long pipeline (buildings started
in times of severe shortages often come on-stream when there is an
excess of space) but also the vitality and future expectations of the
market. Suburban vacancies approach nearly 20 percent, the CBD
equivalent barely 13 percent; yet the thrust of new construction is
still suburban, mainly in development corridors.

The rise to prominence of the suburban growth corridor is the
result of many factors. While precise causal linkages are elusive, we
have attempted to illustrate at least the general parameters in Figure 1. Three initiating factors are important: the evolution of the
American economy to the point where the service sector is the overwhelmingly dominant growth element; federal financial deregula-
tory actions and tax legislation, which provided enormous incentives for real estate investment; and the third-generation impact
of the nation's interstate highway system. These developments
have tended to foster, respectively, intensive metropolitan service

Figure 1. Suburban growth corridors: Rationale.

1. National economic change	generates	Metropolitan service growth
+ Federal tax and regulatory policy	generates	Office overbuilding
+ Third-generation highway system impact	generates	Suburban growth corridor development
2. Scale of overbuilding and development overhanging in the suburban growth corridor	generates	Establishment of future economic infrastructure + Preemption of spatial competition + Slower future development growth

3. The future: The coming of age of the suburbanized economy

growth, massive office construction and overbuilt markets, and suburban growth corridors marked by concentrated office development along metropolitan ring highways.

The scale of overbuilding and the development overhang that have resulted are unprecedented in post–World War II annals; in essence, they represent the establishment of the American economy's future infrastructure. The phenomenon is so substantial that it ensures slower future development growth and the preemption of alternative spatial development competition. The future will be defined by a maturing suburbanized economy with national growth increments increasingly attached to the emerging concentrations.

The new economy

To describe America's economy as service dominated is now a platitude. The sheer level of change, however, is worth reviewing. Agriculture took 300 years to give way in total employment to manufacturing—a passing of the banner that did not occur until World War I. Manufacturing's predominance, in terms of its proportion of non-agricultural jobs, survived only through World War II. By 1980 more Americans were engaged in trading goods than in manufacturing them. And the shifts within the last decade have been even more monumental, with marketers of real estate—and related services as well—limping after the reality.

The rapidity of change is indicated in Table 2, which presents U.S. employment growth by sector for 1976 to 1981 and from 1981 through 1985. The employment categories are proximately based on the *Business Week* (June 1, 1981) segments designed to conceptualize the American economy as five distinct sectors. We have added trade and distribution (basically wholesale and retail trade) as a sixth component.

Table 2. *U.S. employment growth by sector: 1976–1985 (numbers in thousands.)* Source: U.S. Department of Labor, Bureau of Labor Statistics, *Employment and Earnings* (monthly) for original data.

	1976	1981	1985	Change: 1976–1981		Change: 1981–1985	
				Number	Percent	Number	Percent
Total employment	77,731	90,817	96,045	13,086	16.8	5,228	5.8
Old-line industry	18,548	20,306	19,274	1,758	9.5	−1,032	−5.1
High technology	3,074	4,075	4,280	1,001	32.6	205	5.0
Energy	758	1,085	987	327	43.1	−98	−9.0
Services	26,354	33,288	37,961	6,934	26.3	4,673	14.0
Government	15,322	16,408	16,468	1,086	7.1	60	0.4
Trade and distribution	13,675	15,655	17,075	1,980	14.5	1,420	9.1

Note: Data includes only nonfarm payroll employment as of March of the respective years.

The 1976 to 1981 tabulations seemed to point the way to the future. The era shaped by the oil crises spawned a 43 percent increase in energy jobs and a 33 percent gain in high technology. Both of these sectors expanded at greater rates than did services or trade/distribution. Old-line industry had yet to feel the real pinch of the import surge of the 1980s and by 1981 had added more than 1.7 million jobs from the level imposed by the mid-decade recession.

While services and trade dominated the absolute growth increments, all sectors showed fairly robust gains. But the priority targets, based on rapidity of growth, were evident. High technology was the future, energy growth was limited only by natural sites, and funding for synthetic resources was clearly of the highest priority. These would help fuel the locomotive pulling the more modest-paced train of services and trade/distribution activities.

When we turn to the 1981 to 1985 period, however, the future was markedly different. The services and trade sectors accounted for practically all the employment increase. Old-line industry had shrunk by more than 1 million jobs while its expected offset, high technology, expanded by only 200,000. The energy sector, much to the dismay of Texas and the Rocky Mountain states, lost nearly 100,000 jobs. Even government, long viewed as a stable growth sector, barely registered a minimal gain (as the comparatively stagnant Washington residential realty market will attest).

Thus, the growth bases of the late 1970s proved to be highly deceptive as we moved into the middle 1980s. International manufacturing competition—both in old-line industries and high technology—agricultural stagnation and the energy glut have served to narrow the nation's economic growth sectors and their geographic patterning as well. But real estate development has a long gestation period, often reflecting the past rather than the future. This is mirrored in both the location and types of improvements that are undertaken.

The movement to house services—in part by default of other opportunities—came on the scene with enormous vigor at the beginning of the decade and overshot by far the market's absorptive needs. The 1981 Economic Recovery Tax Act was dedicated to revitalizing America's overall industrial infrastructure. In the face of the shift in employment growth, however, it succeeded very largely in generating shelter for clericals.

Tax and regulatory policy

The 1980s have been indelibly marked by changes in various federal tax and regulatory provisions that have served to redirect capital flows to commercial real estate development, particularly the office sector. This is enhanced by the accessing of a whole host of new financial sources—pension funds and corporate treasuries alike, both domestic and overseas. The following are among the more prominent changes that have channeled massive amounts of investment—and speculative—resources into such ventures: the tax write-off provided by 18-year depreciation; the special tax provisions for syndicates and limited real estate partnerships; regulatory changes that removed interest rate ceilings from lending institutions to compete for deposits and financial deregulation provisions that allowed savings and loan associations (the thrifts) to engage in nonresidential lending.

All of these shifts were intended to revitalize the economy, stimulate reindustrialization, save the financially ailing thrift industry and unshackle private enterprise. While unintended consequences are often characteristics of federal policy actions, the result here is particularly unique. In conjunction with changes in the economy, investment became overwhelmingly targeted on office and commercial real estate development. And the latter have been placed along our major freeway arteries.

Highway impacts

The skeletal framework of economic suburbia was unwittingly initiated more than a quarter of a century ago. In the middle 1950s, bulldozers first began what was then probably the largest public works project in history—the 41,000-mile interstate highway system. Originally justified via national defense requirements, it has since served to spatially restructure the American economy.

This reshaping has had three major dimensions that became apparent during successive decades. The first-generation effect was the residential suburbanization that dominated our metropolitan areas in the 1950s and 1960s. The first stages of interstate construction served to facilitate the basic processes at work—the dispersion and decentralization of population and population-serving activities.

As the system drove toward completion it served to alter patterns of regional connectivity, the second major impact. Many parts of the South gained greater accessibility to the broader U.S. economy, providing a major stimulus for the shifting regional fortunes of the 1970s.

The third-generation impact prevailed in the 1980s. The interstates—and equivalent-scale roadways—became the lifelines of the new suburban growth corridors. In part, this represents the rise to full influence of the ring of freeways surrounding virtually every metropolitan area. The earlier impacts were predicated on metropolitan radials (residential suburbanization) and on the long-distance intermetropolitan/interstate components (regional development and integration). But now it is the arteries originally designed to bypass metropolitan centers that have themselves become anchors of intensive development.

The suburban growth zones are certainly not restricted, however, to metropolitan beltways. Radial outgrowth corridors have often emerged, proceeding from the circumferential to an outlying node. And zones have emerged inside the ring roads, usually tied to specialized locations. But it has been the full maturation of the interstate system that has transformed America's economic geography.

The development game

Within this context, it is the development industry that actually shapes the built landscape. One cannot fully comprehend the birth of the suburban growth corridor, or the actual locales of its emergence, without understanding developer behavior. The concepts of legitimacy and the market snake dance are key to the process.

Tax parameters have virtually ensured a large volume of office building construction. Economic changes have reduced alternative opportunities, leaving the national service industries as the remaining target. As one observer has pointed out, developers have shifted from Southwest to Northeast, from downtown to suburbia and from highrise to lowrise. And they often move in seeming lockstep from overbuilt areas to underbuilt ones, only to saturate the market, in turn instigating the search for new ones.

A starting point of the process is the legitimizing of location. Once a major player makes a commitment to a market, the location secures certification—it becomes a legitimate target for the national development community. At the extreme, a market snake dance ensues, with trailing players, desperate to achieve market presence, chasing after the initiators.

The exact triggering mechanism, however, remains difficult to specify. In the Princeton corridor, for example, the mechanism was the university's direct real estate development activity—Forrestal Center—that provided the baseline for the 1980s' explosion.

Other growth zones have been predicated on functional activities. The Washington area's Dulles Access Corridor built up momentum on the basis of federally supported high-tech operations, particularly in defense communications. In contrast, the Fairfield County, Connecticut, and Westchester County, New York, corridors represent mature/diversified markets, initially based on corporate headquarters relocations of the past decade, now fortified by branch office and service entourages. These are just a few of the diversified bases from which the growth corridors emerged. But beyond gestation they have tended to achieve common form as they become immersed in the national development matrix.

Demographic critical mass

Public attention is frequently directed toward unique occurrences at the expense of the modular event. An interstate relocation of credit card services by a Citicorp from New York to South Dakota generates a sea of speculation on the new homogenization of space and time resulting from maturing communications technologies. We would suggest, however, that while there may be a few emulators of this type of locational behavior, at least in the near-term future, this will *not* be a key dimension of America's economic ecology.

The movement of office facilities and high-tech research and development accommodations to suburbia is not only the natural product of transportation evolution, but even more so of the shift of the population's critical mass, both in number and perhaps even more strikingly in socioeconomic characteristics. The labor-intensive character of the American service economy cannot be overlooked in this context.

America's post–World War II residential suburbanization was powerfully fostered by federal policy focussed on housing-enabling mechanisms. The pattern of commuting for work purposes to the central city now involves a decreasing minority of suburbanites. Instead, as suburbia has come of age, there has been an enormous burgeoning of its labor force potential, but it is linked to jobs reasonably proximate to home location.

The two-income household is the rule, not the exception. This requires residential centrality and job choice. Both of these are now available in the suburban growth corridor. The central city's role has been upstaged. One of the key appeals of suburban/metropolitan fringe location versus either central city on the one hand or isolated rural exurbia on the other is the sheer scale and quality of the labor force that can be assembled—and indeed, if necessary, disassembled—without causing much turbulence to the local economy.

These factors were solidifying in the 1970s, courtesy of the third-generation impact of the highway program. When joined in the 1980s by metropolitan service growth and new federal tax legislation, a tendency was transformed into terrifying momentum. And as has been the case so often in modern-day America, the role of the baby boom cannot be discounted. The baby boom was born in suburbia, raised in suburbia, settled in suburbia and now works in suburbia, tales of gentrification and yuppies notwithstanding. Given the dominance of this suburban generation, it is not surprising that its employers would locate accordingly. The suburban growth corridor is intimately linked to the maturation of the baby boom.

Implications

What is the import of this development? It in no way indicates that central city America is going out of business. One only has to look at the new vigor of downtown Baltimore or Philadelphia, to say nothing of New York or Boston, to appreciate this. We would suggest, however, that the sheer scale of suburban office construction is the equivalent of a preemptive strike, limiting the scale of future development. In and of itself, it is sufficient to absorb the office labor force growth predicted for the balance of the decade. In its unrented condition it stands as hardy competition to any additional new construction.

Distressed properties provide bargain rents and the latter are sufficient to dissuade even the most optimistic of risk takers. The physical matrix of the next decade's economy, therefore, is largely set. This will be particularly the case in light of potential tax reform which, at the very least, may include significantly less generous treatment of new office construction.

But the residential sector will exhibit several tendencies. Within the corridors, high-density residential clusters will emerge, while simultaneously the outer metropolitan fringe will be transformed into ruburbia—a hybrid form of rural, exurban and suburban development formats. Overall, the combination of dispersion and increasing corridor density will raise new challenges to both transportation and infrastructure development.

One of the classic theses of central city advocates has suggested that suburbia's increasing density ultimately must force an equivalent infrastructure response. This, in turn, will tend to raise local operating and capital costs, thus reducing one of the competitive disadvantages of core areas. This is a process which is presently underway. The principal infrastructure targets of the next decade will be much more concentrated in the new growth zones than in any other areas. The age of the septic tank is giving way to sophisticated waste treatment facilities, while the growing potency of suburban gridlock will require massive expenditures as well—and this at a time when federal funding in many sectors is rapidly departing the scene.

Complicating forecasts of future growth is a new calculus of developmental politics. There are clear signs of increasing resistance to development, particularly in the most desirable of suburbs. The decade-ago objection of suburban/exurban Greenwich, Connecticut, to commercial proliferation was unique. At the time, it fostered a spillover to Stamford, but now the no-growth response is rapidly becoming much more universal. The recession-born insecurity that spawned aggressive pro-growth strategies is yielding to complacency—and indeed a fear of urbanization.

These latter elements are far from the exclusive purview of suburbia—they are joined in by central cities as well. The last mayoralty contest in Boston—with both major candidates running against an overcommitment to downtown development—is a case in point. Even Houston and Dallas, long the capitals of unquestioned enterprise, are beginning to evidence the same types of resistance.

The developmental pressures for physical infrastructure support in the suburban growth corridors are overwhelming. The physical geometry of the 1990s' economy has been decided. We do not have to invent the future; the tax policy–driven office builders have set it in place.

The Rise of America's Community Development Corporations

Neal R. Peirce and Carol F. Steinbach

From the war in Vietnam to the war on poverty—Sam Smith was in for a shock when he returned to North Philadelphia in 1969 after military duty in Southeast Asia. The neighborhoods he'd known as a boy were in shambles. Scores of refuse-strewn empty lots had been left by urban renewal's bulldozers. The grand old black entertainment street of Columbia Avenue was in a downward spiral triggered by the riots following Martin Luther King's assassination in 1968. Homeowners refused to spend money on their property, expecting to be displaced as nearby Temple University bought up land for potential expansion.

Seventeen years after his return from Vietnam, Sam Smith drives visitors through North Philadelphia. One would have to be callous beyond belief not to be overwhelmed by the crumbling mortar and graffiti, deep poverty and abandonment. The North Philadelphia ghetto is no single pocket of decay. Stretching block after block, it covers a vast expanse of one of America's great cities.

But North Philadelphia is not without its surprises. Suddenly Smith is showing off twenty-three new solar town houses. Pointing to 200 other units of new or rehabilitated housing. Noting some 400 parcels, taken by the city for nonpayment of taxes and now "land banked" for future projects. Talking about community gardens, a thrift store, the start of commercial rehabilitation along Columbia Avenue. And taking visitors to a new trash recycling plant that has created a handful of jobs for hard-core jobless youths plus a source of income for scavenger trash collectors.

Reprinted with permission from Neal R. Peirce and Carol F. Steinbach, *Corrective Capitalism: The Rise of America's Community Development Corporations* (New York: Ford Foundation, 1987). The portion of the book reproduced here was originally entitled "Diamonds in the Rough."

A CDC, the National Temple Non-Profit Corporation, Sam Smith its president, is sparking this development. Begun in 1968 by congregants of the National Temple Baptist Church, it has a rich agenda, ranging from community advocacy to real estate management, block-captain organization to town watch, free food for the hungry (18,000 meals annually) to technical assistance for small businesses.

National Temple is no stranger to failure: not all the projects it has dreamed up have obtained funding. But confidence in this CDC's capacity to deliver has risen so sharply in Philadelphia that in 1986 it received $550,000 for operations, another $1.5 million for projects. Among the multiple sources: Community Development Block Grants, city appropriations, the Catholic Church's Campaign for Human Development, CIGNA, American Express, the Local Initiatives Support Corporation, the Ford Foundation, Pew Memorial Trust, and the Mellon Bank.

What manner of organization tackles the toughest societal problems, plays charity and capitalist and community organizer at the same time, and can manage to bring government, corporate, philanthropic, and religious America all on board?

The answer is the community development corporation. CDCs vary dramatically in their origins, their track records, their styles, their wealth, the types of urban and rural communities they serve. Not all even call themselves CDCs, using instead such varied designations as "neighborhood development organizations" or "economic development corporations." About 99 percent are nonprofit, most often tax-exempt "501(C)3" organizations, which makes it easier to attract foundation and government grants. Commonly, CDCs spin off for-profit arms to do development work or operate profit-making enterprises.

The universe of nonprofit organizations serving the poor is vast, ranging from traditional social service organizations such as United Way to groups with more of a development focus—a category that includes CDCs as well as cooperatives, minority business development programs, and neighborhood housing services. There are no "neat" lines. But the following three characteristics are present in the National Temple Non-Profit Corporation and in fact in all CDCs.

Community control

CDCs sprang out of the neighborhoods, starting in the 1960s when the notion that community residents could define and control development in their communities was considered radical. Twenty-five years and thousands of new CDCs later, this is one element of the "experiment" that is widely regarded as an unqualified success. Control by boards of directors composed primarily of community residents is a virtually immutable constant.

National Temple's fifteen-person board is not untypical. In addition to neighborhood residents, it includes representatives from CIGNA, Bell of Pennsylvania, and the Philadelphia Urban Coalition.

A few CDC boards play a limited, passive, or largely ceremonial role. But that is rare. Most boards are far more active, with members making important contributions to fund raising, community relations, lobbying, and credibility building. In many CDCs, board members also play a major role in setting policy and choosing projects; in some, board members are involved in actual project implementation.

Quite a few CDCs have created subsidiary boards or special advisory committees composed of local business and political leaders. The granddaddy of CDCs, Brooklyn, N.Y.'s Bedford-Stuyvesant Restoration Corporation, pioneered this approach. Its operational arm, the Restoration Corporation, administers overall CDC operations under the directorship of a local board. A companion organization, the Development and Services Corporation, contributes business contacts and expertise. Its directors over the years have included such corporate and political leaders as former Treasury Secretary C. Douglas Dillon, former Senators Jacob Javits and Robert Kennedy, CBS chief William S. Paley, Chemical Bank Vice Chairman Richard K. LeBlond, and business magnate Benno C. Schmidt, Sr.

It's not unknown for debilitating fights to break out among CDC board members or between boards and staff. Some tensions, it would seem, are almost inevitable. But by and large, relations are harmonious.

Economic development

Every CDC undertakes economic development projects. Most are of a "hard" development character—constructing or rehabilitating housing and commercial real estate, starting businesses, creating jobs for local residents. Most CDCs also have a "softer" component more directly related to human services—child care and elder care, skills training, home-ownership counseling, summer camps, health screening, drug and alcohol abuse programs, for example. Whatever the development mix, the goal of every CDC is the immediate relief of severe economic, social, and physical distress—and, eventually, wider regeneration of the community.

Targeting

All CDCs focus their activities in a clearly defined geographic area encompassing a high concentration of low-income people. This may mean a heavily disadvantaged, underclass urban neighborhood such as North Philadelphia, the South Bronx, or Watts in Los Angeles, where CDCs strive to rebuild dilapidated housing, to rekindle a spark of economic vitality, to reverse residents' overwhelming sense of negativism and isolation, and to send a signal to the community outside that the decline has "bottomed out."

Other CDCs focus on trying to stem decline in ailing working-class neighborhoods in danger of further deterioration. Quite often the chosen method is to combine "hard" development with CDC-sponsored programs to promote stabilization through home ownership. Consider the Northeast Denver Housing Center, in a single-family residential neighborhood, roughly two-thirds black, an area interspersed with commercial strips populated by liquor stores, fast-food outlets, pawn shops, and bars. Twelve neighborhood groups started the Housing Center in 1982. They prevailed on John Stovall, retired after thirty years' civilian service with the Air Force, to serve as director.

Stovall—black, businesslike, indefatigable—scraped up subsidies from the city and state governments, the Piton Foundation (Denver's prime funder of neighborhood-based projects), local banks, and later the Ford Foundation. By 1987, the Housing Center had provided counseling to more than 1,500 first-time home buyers, including information on how to get a mortgage or remove a blot from one's credit rating. It had assisted 600 homeowners behind on mortgage payments and in danger of foreclosure, negotiating with banks and helping some residents obtain small tide-over loans from the city's housing agency. Through its buyer incubation program, the Housing Center had instructed tenants in its own units on how to raise a down payment and care for their own homes. And it had bought fifty-eight HUD- and VA-foreclosed houses and readied them for low-income purchasers.

An alternative CDC focus may be to try to restore vitality to deteriorating shopping and commercial strips. A prime example: East Liberty Development Inc. (ELDI) in Pittsburgh. The city prevailed on the local Chamber of Commerce to start ELDI in 1979. But the real spark for this CDC came from an aggressive branch manager of the Mellon bank, who dragooned East Liberty business, church, and civic leaders into his basement for a decisive meeting on how the new CDC could begin turning things around. The challenge was formidable. East Liberty's array of once-thriving neighborhood stores and retail chains had been steadily hemorrhaging, down from 242 establishments in 1963 to only 98 in 1977. A grand $68 million city-sponsored urban renewal "experiment" in the 1960s—erecting traffic barriers to turn East Liberty into an area of pedestrian shopping malls—had backfired, repelling the neighborhood's working-class clientele, and making it virtually impossible for the heavy flow of downtown commuters to get to East Liberty stores.

With major financial support provided by the city, the Ford Foundation, the Howard Heinz Endowment, and the Mellon Bank Foundation, ELDI launched an aggressive campaign to lure businesses back to East Liberty. Its approach: a combination of hard-nosed promotion tactics and hands-on business assistance, targeted to large developers and small enterprises alike. ELDI services range from writing business plans and packaging financing to help with advertising, site selection, job training and recruitment, even exporting goods abroad. By 1987, 120 new businesses had opened in the neighborhood, creating 1,200 jobs. Four major new private developments were completed or under way—two new shopping centers, the conversion of an abandoned warehouse into loft-style condominiums, the rehab of an old department store. The city resurfaced major roads and tore down the traffic barriers. East Liberty businesses reported their best sales months ever in 1986.

Some CDCs concentrate on restoring and preserving housing for poor people in neighborhoods undergoing middle-class "gentrification." In Richmond, Va., a four-year-old CDC—the Task Force for Historic Preservation and the Minority Community—is targeting its efforts on Jackson Ward, one of the most historic black neighborhoods in America. For inspiration and advice, the Task Force has looked to Savannah, Ga., where dramatic results are being achieved by the Savannah Landmark Rehabilitation Project, a nonprofit alliance of twenty-three white and black leaders founded by Leopold Adler II, an investment banker. Savannah Landmark in the mid-1970s adopted a breathtaking goal: to purchase and restore for low-income black tenants 600 of the 1,200 apartments and houses in the "Victorian District"—a forty-five-block area of wood-frame gingerbread houses fallen victim to slum landlords and disrepair. A decade later, hundreds of homes had been rehabilitated for poor Savannahans, cheek-by-jowl with the anticipated middle-class gentrification. From the houses' exteriors, it is virtually impossible to know the occupants' income status.

CDCs are not just an urban phenomenon. Some of the largest and oldest CDCs operate in rural areas, many covering a wide territory. The nineteen-year-old Community Enterprise Development Corporation of Alaska, for example, promotes rural development throughout the entire breadth of the country's largest state. Mississippi Action for Community Education targets its wide array of programs on forty counties in the Mississippi-Arkansas Delta region. The Mountain Association for Community Economic Development (MACED), with headquarters in Berea, Ky., has a target area spanning Central Appalachia. The Northern Community Investment Corporation in St. Johnsbury, Vt., focuses its development activities on the 185,000 residents of six impoverished rural counties in Vermont's "Northeast Kingdom" and New Hampshire's "North Country."

CDCs' size and scope

If one looks for a U.S.-wide focus on where CDCs are most likely to be found, the answers (with many exceptions) are: Especially prevalent in older cities of the Northeast and the Midwest. A few in major western cities. In a rural context, east of the Mississippi. The

CDC movement has with a few very notable exceptions made less headway in the Great Plains, the Pacific Northwest, or in most southern cities.

Nationally, Boston and Chicago boast the most well-developed CDC networks, not just because each has a large number of CDCs, but also because of the advanced partnerships CDCs in these two cities have forged with local government and the business community. There are perhaps 100 community-based development groups in Chicago, a city with a tradition of neighborhood organizing, tough advocacy, and success at drawing city hall and private corporations into neighborhood issues. (Some of the heavy flow of capital into Chicago CDCs in the 1980s is the result of threatened legal action against banks under the 1977 Community Reinvestment Act.)

The strength of the CDC movement in Boston, on the other hand, is in no small part a reflection of the strong state support for CDCs initiated by Governor Michael Dukakis in the late 1970s. Since 1981 the number of Massachusetts CDCs has mushroomed from twelve to around seventy, about half of them in Boston.

Other cities with an advanced or growing CDC presence include New York, Philadelphia, Pittsburgh, Cleveland, Denver, Washington, D.C., Hartford, Miami, Indianapolis, St. Louis, Los Angeles, Minneapolis, Baltimore, Newark, Kansas City, San Francisco, Oakland, Cincinnati, Seattle, and Providence.

The more one examines CDCs, the more their infinite variety comes into focus. Although all try to assist less affluent Americans, the immediate target populations they serve vary broadly—Americans of every racial and ethnic stripe, women, farmers, American Indians, welfare recipients, small-business owners, juveniles, the homeless.

Moreover, the size and scope of CDCs vary as much as those of conventional businesses. Chicanos Por La Causa, organized in 1969 by a group of young Hispanic leaders in South Phoenix, now provides statewide service and has a staff of more than 100. Boston's Inquilinos Boricuas en Accion (Puerto Rican Tenants in Action) owns more than $50 million worth of real estate holdings in the city's South End, housing some 2,500 low-income Bostonians. The Community Enterprise Development Corporation of Alaska, through its wholly owned management company and subsidiaries, has annual gross sales of over $60 million.

But these are the exceptions. Most CDCs have only a few paid employees and operate on relative shoestrings. They rent space in modest offices; they rely on donated services from accountants, lawyers, and corporations; their yearly budgets probably average no higher than $200,000. Lucky is the CDC with more assets than a couple of typewriters, a computer, a copier, a coffee machine. And lots of folding chairs.

Revitalizing the Mahoning Valley

Terry F. Buss and Roger Vaughan

The Mahoning Valley is located midway between Cleveland and Pittsburgh in northeast Ohio. The metropolitan area of 500,000 people includes the cities of Youngstown (pop. 105,000) in Mahoning County and Warren (pop. 55,000) in Trumbull County.

For nearly 50 years, the Youngstown/Warren area was a world center for basic steel manufacturing. At its peak in the 1950s, nearly 50,000 workers were employed in primary metals.

The dominance of steel employment changed on 19 September 1977, when Youngstown Sheet and Tube Company, one of the nation's largest steel producers, announced that it was permanently closing its Campbell Works. Shortly after the announcement, nearly 5,000 workers became redundant. The closing of Sheet and Tube augured the subsequent closing of steel mills throughout the United States and in many other industrialized countries. From 1976 to 1986, nearly 40,000 jobs were lost in the Mahoning Valley, 21,000 in primary metals and another 19,000 in blast furnace and basic steel occupations.

In a single decade, the Mahoning Valley lost the core of its economy—its traditional source of economic growth. Despite the gravity of the problems, the local response was fragmentary and misplaced. Local agencies tried to replace steel with other durable goods manufacturers, without realizing that this sector will not provide the basis of growth in the future. They were preoccupied with bricks and mortar although it is human capital investments that, increasingly, are determining the success of development.

Dissatisfaction with a decade of failed development plans has

Adapted with permission from *Environment and Planning C*, volume 5, 1987, issue 4. *Environment and Planning C* is a publication of Pion Limited, London.

led to the design of a more diversified and people-oriented strategy detailed in the pages that follow. The strategy is organized around five goals: (1) rebuilding the local entrepreneurial tradition; (2) strengthening the existing economic base; (3) creating opportunity for the economically disadvantaged; (4) improving the quality of public services; and (5) improving the quality of life. Responsibilities for carrying out the specific policies spelled out in the strategy will be shared among local governments, nonprofit agencies, the private sector, and Youngstown State University. Without the involvement of all these parties, the strategy would fail.

The strategy deliberately does not pursue "target industries," because forecasts cannot be made with sufficient accuracy; "enterprise zones," since enormous subsidies have been shown to be ineffective; "public loan funds," because the public sector's track record in picking firms to lend to is poor; "high technology," because private developers will prove more adept; or "industrial recruitment," because it, too, has already failed many times. The approach offered here is less traditional but more firmly derived from a model of economic development that centers on entrepreneurial decision-making.

A model for economic development

What is a community pursuing when it makes economic development its top priority? What is economic development?[1] The definition of economic development depends on the interests and intentions of the definer. To many organizations in the Mahoning Valley it has meant the growth of jobs—a visible measure and one that appears necessary in communities suffering chronic unemployment. Yet, if jobs are the criteria, how should we treat the adoption of new, laborsaving equipment, or the expansion of capital-intensive industries at the expense of labor-intensive ones? How much should we spend to attract a job, and how can we be sure that the enterprise creating the jobs is viable?

Other developers regard high technology firms as the core of development today. Yet the major contribution of technology is not through the much-sought-after firms manufacturing new devices but through the adoption of modern technology by existing firms. Others measure a community's development strength by the number of companies that have been induced to move in from elsewhere or the number of branches opened locally. They ignore the vital importance of new businesses and new products. None of these definitions is sufficiently broad to encompass all the facets of the process that must be explored in order to develop a comprehensive and effective development strategy.

At its broadest and simplest, economic development is the creation of wealth. Wealth is the community's capacity to produce goods and services of value to its residents. This includes those goods and services that are bought and sold—fabricated metal, banking, auto repairs, and movies—as well as those that are less tangible but nonetheless valuable—recreational opportunities, public safety, and clean air. Although wealth is difficult to define, it yields important policy implications.

Pursuing opportunities Economic opportunities exist, and new ones are continually being created because no one knows all there is to know about what types of goods and services can be produced, about different ways of making them, or about all the markets where goods and services can be sold. A new idea might profitably capture consumers' spending. Science, engineering, people's imagination, and changes in economic circumstances are continually creating new opportunities. Events which to many of us seem harmful—like the increase in energy costs in the 1970s—create opportunities as well as destroying them—from a boom in radar detectors, to a whole industry in energy conserving devices. Economic development is a continuous process of discovery—of new items that consumers value, new and cheaper ways of making things, or of new markets.

Communities like the Mahoning Valley, where development lags, rarely lack opportunities. Instead, they lack the capacity to "harvest" opportunities locally because of the absence of an entrepreneurial tradition or because of barriers to entrepreneurship such as the lack of capital, the weight of long-held tradition, or restrictions on new business activities.

In all communities, new firms are continually being formed, even during poor economic conditions. Youngstown has experienced a very low rate of business formation, but it is not zero. At the height of the economic collapse new metal-fabricating firms were successfully begun. Those new enterprises that survive will provide jobs and wealth for the community in the future. It is easy to overlook their contribution because they start small and unnoticed, whereas the plants that are closing are usually large and well known. The replacement of the old by the new is an important way in which a community adjusts to its changing economic environment.

Taking risks Pursuing opportunities means taking risks. To test the viability of new ideas, to develop ways of producing and marketing those ideas, and to test their managerial skills, people must invest their time and, usually, their money as well. Those people who became entrepreneurs have the most to gain by the success of their venture. They may act independently or they may be working for a large organization that rewards individual initiative.

Each decision that contributes to development requires an enormous amount of information. The modern economy is organized to allow participants to specialize in the acquisition and use of information. Through financial institutions people can invest their money in an almost infinite variety of instruments, varying in risk and expected return.

The image that many people have of entrepreneurship is of an engineering graduate becoming a millionaire by "going public" with a firm producing arcane computer hardware or software. Even in Silicon Valley this is the exception and not the rule, and in the rest of the country it is extremely rare. Entrepreneurship encompasses a much wider range of activities, including self-employment, inventing and marketing new goods and services, and nurturing a new company. There is no typical entrepreneur—they can be found among all regions, all races, and among men and women. The unemployed and those with low incomes frequently turn to entrepreneurship—especially if the prospects for return to their previous job, or any job, are dim. The late Albert Shapero devoted a lifetime to studying entrepreneurs. He found that negative factors were responsible for almost half of new business formations.[2]

The number of active entrepreneurs in a community depends on the rewards anticipated from the pursuit of opportunities, the strength of the local entrepreneurial tradition, the availability of capital, and the absence of artificial barriers to entering different professions and industries.

Investing   Translating an innovation into wealth requires investments which include:

Business capital. Business firms invest in plant, equipment, inventory, research and development, marketing, and, frequently, in political lobbying.

Human capital. Individuals seek to enhance their future earnings and to acquire the skills needed to pursue entrepreneurial opportunities by investing in education and training (classroom and on-the-job) and by moving to areas with better employment opportunities.

Public infrastructure. Local, state, and federal governments are currently spending about one hundred billion dollars a year to restore, maintain, and expand the nation's public works—roads, bridges, water supply and treatment, flood control, and education facilities.

These investments are made by most members of the community. Yet the development policies that have been pursued in Youngstown have focused on only a small number of decisions—an aircraft manufacturer's decision to locate locally, a steel plant, or a federal building. They have ignored the vast majority of investment decisions and suffered the fate of any investor who places all of his resources in a few assets. The strategy outlined below is much more diversified.

Funds available for investment are limited. They are allocated among businesses, individuals, and governments for competing projects by the capital market. Growth proceeds most rapidly if the investments with the highest expected payoffs are funded first. This basic rule was ignored by those providing subsidies to the many failed ventures in the Mahoning Valley. But real profitability is not the only factor that shapes investments. Tax and regulatory policies, the distribution of wealth and income among members of the community, and political influences on public (and sometimes on private) investments all shape the way funds flow through the capital market. An important part of any strategy building is to identify the impediments to the operation of the capital market which redirect investment funds in ways that are inconsistent with stated policy goals. The appropriate treatment may be then to find ways of removing or reducing the distortion.

If individuals or private firms do not have information as accurate as that available to public agencies, then appropriate treatment may be for the latter to play some part in the capital market—either by making the information broadly available to potential entrepreneurs (a role undertaken by some state university systems, for example) or by directly financing certain types of investment (as in the case of human capital).

Conflict Development not only creates wealth, it also redistributes wealth. Not everyone gains more than they lose by it. As consumers, we all gain from the wider choices and lower prices of goods and services. But as resource owners, stockholders, and employees we may win or lose. If the company we have invested in or work for is beaten in the marketplace by other enterprises, we may suffer losses on investments or loss of income, against which the new products will seem small compensation.

Every step forward in the development process is incremental. Each successful entrepreneurial venture displaces existing jobs. Sometimes the displacement is direct and obvious—a new restaurant that leads to the closing of an old one nearby. Sometimes it is less obvious—the successful new enterprise making home-exercise equipment attracts consumers' spending away from other activities—from bowling to visits to the local fitness center. Because consumers are choosing freely among these alternatives, we know that the new expenditure pattern represents an improvement in a community's aggregate wealth, even though some members of the community are worse off.

Those losing from a particular phase of development may try to use the political process to recoup some of their losses—a loan for an ailing company, for example. Even if those gaining outnumber those losing and the benefits of development outweigh the costs, those harmed may be better organized and more concentrated geographically. This may enable them to use the political process to seek legislative redress. Preserving existing businesses is often attractive politically. Yet, in the longer run, as Youngstown's experience shows, these policies may slow the emergence of new enterprises and discourage entrepreneurs with better skills. "The ultimate result," as English philosopher Herbert Spencer has said, "of shielding men from the effects of folly, is to fill the world with fools."[3]

An action agenda

The strategy for economic recovery in the Mahoning Valley focuses on five main objectives:

Rebuilding the entrepreneurial environment. Much of the development must come from those people already living within the region. The effect of relying on one industry to provide most of the economic opportunities for three generations must be overcome by educating people about the importance of entrepreneurs and of assisting start-ups.

Strengthening existing businesses. Many existing firms need assistance to adapt to new products and new markets. However, providing public financial support to troubled enterprises will weaken rather than strengthen the local economic base.

Creating economic opportunity. Many dislocated workers, working poor, and welfare recipients will need targeted policies and programs to extend opportunity to all potential members of the workforce. These programs should complement rather than detract from the underlying economic strategy.

Improving public services. In the long run, the most important economic development function of the state and local government is to ensure that the education system turns out high-quality graduates, that public infrastructure is well maintained, and that all public services are efficiently provided.

Improving the quality of life. Although economic development policy traditionally focuses on the business climate, diversifying the region's economy will depend more on its ability to attract or retain people rather than on enterprises.

Perhaps the most important caveat to make in developing this agenda is that there are limits to what can be achieved through state and local government initiatives, even with the support of local business leadership. The Mahoning Valley will continue to be dominated by events determined in the national or even the international policy arena. There is no single policy or program that will generate hundreds of jobs, at least not in the short run. Most economic opportunities start small, with growing entrepreneurial activity. Many fail, and those that do succeed may take several years to prove themselves. However, with no collective action, the region may suffer much deeper and more prolonged economic stagnation.

An economic development program should be regarded as an investment portfolio to which the rules of prudent investment apply; *first*, resources should be diversified as widely as possible among assets whose individual risk is independent of the others; *second*, other investors should be brought in whenever possible to take advantage of pooled expertise and resources; *third*, portfolio managers should never enter an investment without having identified a way out; and *fourth*, successful policies yield returns in the long term and should not be treated as short-term speculations.

Rebuilding the entrepreneurial environment   The Mahoning Valley has lost some of that entrepreneurial tradition that was present late in the last century when new enterprises laid the foundation of the steel industry. To recover, local residents must relearn how to create jobs by making use of their own talents and resources.

Potential entrepreneurs exist locally, but what sets of policies or programs will actuate potential entrepreneurs? Public programs cannot create entrepreneurs, but they can provide an environment in which entrepreneurship flourishes.

This strategy offers a four-pronged attack to improve the entrepreneurial climate: *first*, a variety of "consciousness raising" programs about self-employment and the economics of entrepreneurship will be introduced into area vocational, high school, community college, and university curricula—not to teach people how to become entrepreneurs, but to change existing attitudes about the possibility of entrepreneurship. *Second*, an awards and recognition program for entrepreneurs will be established to provide mentors or role models to entrepreneurial aspirants. *Third*, a program to train entrepreneurs will be offered, but unlike most such efforts, by experienced entrepreneurs who will be compensated only if their assistance leads to successful business start-ups. *Fourth*, public regulations which inhibit competition as a way of protecting existing businesses will be reviewed with an eye toward their reduction or elimination.

Strengthening existing industry   Rapid change in local economies is reflected not only in plant closings, but in the weakening of the competitive position of surviving firms. To improve the competitive edge of local firms, new technologies must be adopted, new skills acquired, foreign markets penetrated, and foreign competitors resisted.

Public programs to strengthen local industry are often no more than subsidies to "bail out" or prolong the life of failing firms. In the long run, these firms either absorb the markets of other firms or, through subsidies, waste public resources.

This strategy includes only policies which will lead to effective adaptation. For example, many small businesses do not have the research and development facilities to discover and test new ideas for products or production methods. Youngstown State University will establish a technology-transfer program in which new technologies will be shared with small businesses in the area. One such activity might include matching special skills of the YSU engineering faculty with applied research needed by small businesses.

As another program, either in a consortium with other Ohio cities or in contract with existing out-of-state programs, the region will establish an export-assistance program, funded in part by the US Department of Commerce, which could help small business to (1) identify overseas markets, (2) arrange financing, (3) conduct international marketing, and (4) secure insurance against cargo loss.

Creating opportunity Too often, special groups in the labor force—discouraged workers, working poor, welfare recipients, unskilled youth, and the elderly—have suffered because programs targeted to their needs sometimes conflict with broader economic development policies. Urban renewal programs which devastated poor neighborhoods without improving anyone's fortunes are a poignant example. Although there is a tradition in economics that assisting the poor means sacrificing economic growth, the tradeoff is not necessary. A more entrepreneurial environment will be of special value to the disadvantaged.

Three initiatives are envisioned in this part of the strategy. *First,* people receiving welfare benefits will be offered opportunities to achieve independence through a variety of training, education, and work-experience initiatives. *Second,* the gap between high school and the job market will be narrowed by improving the responsiveness of schools, rewarding at-risk students who stay in school, and teaching job-search techniques. *Third,* an adult remedial education program for the illiterate and poorly educated will be offered and motivated by vigorous marketing and the provision of financial incentives.

Improving public services The most important contribution the public sector can make to economic development is the delivery of the right services, efficiently, and at a reasonable tax-price. Without this commitment by city and state, all of the other incentives and programs are jeopardized.

Our strategy initially focuses only on two broad types of services—education and capital planning/budgeting, which are critical for economic development. Public services can be improved only if the accountability of public agencies is strengthened by measuring their performance.

The strategy calls for the measurement and publication of placement rates and earnings of graduates from the postsecondary vocational education system, to be used as a basis for informed choice by students and to make the system more accountable for its performance. Each term, students seeking to acquire a marketable skill must choose courses or colleges with less information than is available to the buyer of a small air conditioner. Our strategy assumes that the education system will become more responsive to the labor market if performance is measured.

Another area concerns capital planning and budgeting. The infrastructure of a region is not usually considered an economic development resource, except in rare cases when a new firm or industrial park requires highways, lighting, or sewers. But the public infrastructure is the system which makes possible the private production of goods and services, and in other cases directly affects quality of life when related to parks, museums, golf courses, and the like. The strategy calls for a complete overhaul of the capital planning and budgeting system now used in municipalities in the region.

Quality of life Quality of life and urban amenities are becoming important as economic development issues. A region's ability to attract and retain educated people is as important as its ability to attract firms. Such amenities are seen not as the by-product of economic endeavor, but indeed are a major goal achievable through development.

As with public services, quality of life is multifaceted. In this strategy, policymaking has focused in part on housing as an issue. Specifically, the strategy provides detailed guidelines on where and how public monies should be invested, especially under the CDBG housing rehabilitation and demolition program. An important aspect of the program is to stabilize neighborhoods.

Another quality-of-life issue addressed is the provision of human services to the disadvantaged. Under the strategy, public (such as welfare) and private (such as United Way) agencies are working together to identify community-level needs, to reallocate budget-resources needs, and to eliminate duplication and fragmentation where possible. In addition, alternative private-sector surrogates for public services are recommended as a way of becoming more responsive to needs.

1. R. Vaughan, R. Pollard, and B. Dyer, *The Wealth of States: Policies for a Dynamic Economy* (Washington, D.C.: Council of State Policy and Planning Agencies, 1986).
2. A. Shapero, "The Entrepreneurial Event," in C. A. Kent, ed., *The En-* vironment for Entrepreneurship (Lexington, MA: Lexington Books, 1984).
3. Herbert Spencer, *Essays, Volume 3. State Tampering with Money and Banks* (1891).

Monitoring and Evaluating the Economic Development Program

David R. Kolzow

The role of strategic planning

Strategic planning has become a "hot item" in the field of economic development as hundreds of communities across the country have "discovered" this process. Economic development consultants have changed career direction to become strategic planning consultants. What was once a corporate planning process is being rapidly modified and adapted to the nuances of community economic development. Communities, like the corporations who have used strategic planning for years, are recognizing the process for the many benefits it offers. Its merit lies in the fact that it systematically identifies the assets and liabilities of the area, determines opportunities for growth, gives a sense of direction to local programs so that growth can be achieved, and provides a framework for the evaluation and modification of the economic development program.

It is this last aspect on which this article will focus. Far too often, the evaluation of the local economic development and/or marketing activity gets shortchanged in the overall program. Excitement is generated by local leadership in the planning process, but not enough attention is paid to carrying out or modifying the plan. It is the evaluation process that enables an organization to determine if it is achieving the results it expects, and, if not, why not—and accordingly to make changes in its program.

Accountability

Sooner or later, every economic development and marketing organization has to deal with the issue of accountability. Accountability

Reprinted by permission of the American Economic Development Council from *Economic Development Review* (Summer 1987).

to the board of directors, accountability to local leadership, accountability to the community. The question of "what have you accomplished" is inevitable. Money is spent, staff time is consumed, resources are allocated. All for what?

This question can be best answered by placing the issue of accountability within the framework of the strategic planning process. To begin with, an economic development program that is developed using this process would be founded on a clear set of goals and objectives. The local economic development organization first needs to know what it wants to accomplish so that it can determine the best and most cost-effective methods to reach its objectives. But, more importantly, the organization also needs to know if it has accomplished its goals and objectives, and change its program as necessary to achieve its desired results. Without explicit goals and objectives and set procedures in place for reviewing and evaluating progress, it is difficult to determine whether or not the economic development program has been effective.

Far too often, the economic development organization attempts to equate activity with progress in its efforts to respond to the issue of accountability. The annual report is full of figures, such as the number of inquiries, number of direct mail letters sent, number of prospects handled, number of meetings held, etc. But what do all these numbers and activities mean? What has been accomplished in terms of the economic growth and development of the community?

If a board of directors or the community leadership wants their economic development organization to demonstrate results, then a strategic planning process should be used. The strategic plan, if approached properly, defines what the community would like to achieve by identifying goals and objectives. The goals and objectives, which reflect the resources, desires, and needs of the community as a whole, then become the foundation for the plan of action, otherwise known as the work program.

The work program

The work program is the means by which the strategic plan is implemented and results are achieved and evaluated. Once the economic development organization has a clear sense of where the community *wants* to go and is *able* to go, it is possible to formulate specific tasks and actions that will move the organization and the community in that direction.

In essence, the work program consists of a series of strategic actions, or projects, that need to be accomplished. Each strategic action/project is a series of related tasks that an economic development organization undertakes that are directed toward a specific objective and that are completed within a specific timeframe. This project has intended results, staff commitments, budget allocations, and a time schedule. Obviously, the more explicit these are, the better. Each project has or should have one person responsible for its successful completion. In most community organizations, the director of the economic development organization is the person responsible for all of the economic development projects. These may include media advertising, public relations, brochure development, business retention, small business assistance, and entrepreneurial programs.

Program/project management

Effective management is as important to the success of the economic development program as is a creative plan. Many creative and exciting programs have failed for lack of implementation. For example, an economic development and marketing organization may have an accurate list of target industries well-suited to the community, but unless action is taken to contact these industries very little is likely to happen. The work program may define the actions that should be taken to move the overall program forward, but forward movement generally does not occur without effective management.

Implementing a project that is based on a well-designed work program is much easier than implementing one which is poorly designed. As a result of the work program, a project manager is also able to adjust the performance of the project in response to the expectations of his or her board of directors or other community leaders. Adjustment can also be made in response to other environmental factors such as competitive conditions, changes in the local business climate or local infrastructure, and other unforeseen events or conditions.

Project evaluation

At the beginning of a project, the economic development organization will have a set of expectations for its performance and its results. If these expectations are based upon clearly defined goals and specific objectives, or targets, it is possible to chart and monitor the actions or projects to determine how well they are meeting expectations and to make adjustments as necessary to ensure the meeting of these expectations.

The evaluation of the economic development effort has three dimensions: to monitor progress, to assess performance, and to determine the level of impact. The nature of the information needed depends on the purpose of the evaluation. For example, the information needed for evaluating the progress of a project is different than what is needed for determining the level of impact of the project. However, all three types of evaluation have value in managing the work program and its projects.

Monitoring progress   The purpose of the monitoring effort is to determine whether specific actions and activities were achieved. A key step in monitoring is to compare the current status of a project with an agreed upon schedule of time, expenditures, and results. Obviously, for such monitoring to take place, it is essential that good records be kept by the staff involved in the project. Activity needs to be documented.

A project analysis worksheet, or time task chart, should be constructed for each project. This worksheet focuses on the steps or tasks to be accomplished. (Within the context of a project, a task is any specific activity with a well-defined beginning and end, and a more or less predictable duration and cost.) For each step or task, specific staff are assigned, the number of man-hours are estimated, the date for completion is specified, and the amount of budget allocated is determined.

As the program proceeds, progress should be noted on this worksheet or chart and matched with the tasks and key dates spelled out in the work plan. The more clearly the work plan is stated, the easier the task of setting up a chart for monitoring progress.

Dozens of project management software packages are now available for personal computers to aid in the monitoring process. PERT (Program Evaluation and Review Technique) charts and Gantt charts can be readily produced and periodically modified. PERT charts are used in project management to show the relationship and dependencies between tasks leading up to completion of a project. PERT analysis doesn't necessarily concern itself with how long the individual tasks or activities in a project take, but the order in which those activities have to occur for successful completion of the project. Gantt charts are basically timeliness in a variety of graphic formats to show how long activities within a given project should take.

Project management software is especially useful for managing projects that involve a number of tasks, deadlines ("milestones" in project management jargon), and resources such as people and money. The advantage of using a software program is the dynamic scheduling ability it provides. For example, it takes into account how the completion of one task is dependent on the completion of another. It aids the manager by providing a visualization of schedules. It can also help the manager communicate more effectively. Printouts can show the status of projects to the board of directors or be used to create presentation graphics. And, like spreadsheets, project management software can be used as a "what-if" tool to project the impact of delays or revisions, or to try out plans on-screen before implementing them. For instance, a manager could determine how much overtime will be necessary to bring a project in on schedule if one stage gets behind by a week.

The ultimate purpose of this first type of evaluation is not to discover how well your project is succeeding. The purpose is to be able to revise and adapt the project, if necessary, to new developments so that it can succeed. The monitoring of results at each stage allows necessary changes to be made. Even if the plan works like clockwork, the knowledge that targets have been reached and the understanding of what needs to be achieved next are certain to boost staff morale and performance.

Evaluating performance   The second basic type of evaluation is keyed to the performance of those responsible for carrying out the work plan and the specific projects. The nature of the review of staff performance depends on for whom the evaluation is being done. Is it for the professional, so that he/she can improve his/her performance and be more effective? Is it for the board of directors to demonstrate overall staff effectiveness? Is it for the economic developer as the manager of the program so that he/she can determine what and how well the staff is doing? Is it for the leaders of the community so that they will support the efforts? Is it for the community as a whole so that they will better understand the purpose of the economic development effort? Obviously, the kind of information one seeks for the evaluation will vary considerably depending upon the purpose for which the evaluation will be used.

The appraisal of individual staff performance is a personnel issue, and as such will not be covered in this article. The concern here is the evaluation of the effectiveness of the staff and the projects, and whether they are meeting the goals and objectives set forth in the economic development plan. The issue is the results that are being achieved. What is working and what isn't working? What could be done to improve the system? Are inquiries being properly responded to? Are telephone followups being done effectively? Is the advertising generating a satisfactory level of response? Are prospects being handled correctly? Are the brochures generating a favorable response? Does a different approach need to be used with the direct mailings?

Each project and task within the project has its own set of performance criteria. If the projects are defined properly to begin with, it will not be difficult to develop performance criteria. These criteria, or standards, should represent specific values that can be measured. They may be certain levels of performance regarded as satisfactory by those knowledgeable in the field. In some cases, outside input from another professional may be necessary to keep the evaluation as objective as possible.

At completion of the project or of a set of tasks, the performance reviews present the project manager with an excellent opportunity to provide recognition to project team members. These forms of recognition might include letters of appreciation, plaques or certificates commemorating the individual's contribution, written articles in the organization's newsletter, press releases to the local newspaper, or a luncheon or banquet. The purpose of the recognition is to provide feedback for an assignment or task that has been done exceptionally well. Recognition helps motivate staff members toward improved levels of performance. Since feedback is sometimes negative, position recognition brings more balance to communications.

Measuring impact   The final aspect of evaluation focuses on the impact of the individual projects or on the economic development program as a whole. This is a "so what?" approach. It is easy to get caught up in an evaluation numbers game that documents hours spent on projects contacted, letters sent, dollars spent. Ultimately, the question should be asked, "What does it all mean?"

In this context, three types of questions need to be addressed:

Are the organizational goals correct in terms of: (1) meeting the immediate and long-term economic development needs and opportunities of the community; (2) implementing the economic development program within existing constraints and resources?

Given specific goals and objectives, have local resources been used efficiently in the implementation of the program? Specifically: (1) Are the strategies and projects appropriate? (2) Could more have been achieved by using some other set of strategies or projects? (3) Was the program headed in the right direction in terms of the goals and strategies, but was it not implemented correctly? (4) If so, was the organization or management of the projects inadequate, or did the staff lack competency in technical or political skills?

Given the resources available, could a greater impact have been created in terms of the goals and objectives?

The ability to measure the impact of an economic development program is dependent upon the ability to measure change in the community, and to relate that change to action. This change can be in the number of businesses attracted, the number of new business formations, the number of firms retained or that have expanded locally, the loss or gain of jobs, the rise or fall in the local unemployment rate, the increase or decrease in occupancy rates, etc. Certainly, a good economic development program is one that is as directed to encouraging the growth of the existing base of business and industry in the community as it is to attracting new operations.

This information should be more than quantitive. Numbers alone do not fully describe the changes occurring in an area. Labor attitudes, labor-management relations, quality of educational and training programs, the regulatory environment, and quality-of-life are just some of the important aspects of local economic development that have to be analyzed on a more subjective basis. Qualitative change can be documented through case studies, or specific examples of successes. Firms can be interviewed to determine the role of the economic development effort in the business location or expansion decision.

Conclusion

Obviously, there is a cost in time and staff in gathering the type of information just described. Certainly, practical limits will exist as to how much information be can acquired. However, failure to document the impact of the economic development programs of an organization could lead to serious questions as to the value of the entire economic development program.

One word of warning. When one sets up objectives or targets, try to avoid stating the number of new jobs or firms that will be added to the community. Although it is useful from a planning standpoint to have an idea of how many jobs are needed to bring employment rates to an acceptable level, or how much new business investment is needed to increase the tax base to the point where it could provide for local needs, one's role as an economic development and marketing professional doesn't give one direct control in the business location decisions that lead to these results. The specific statement of numbers is likely come back to haunt one at year-end evaluation if these numbers have not been achieved. Certainly, while one does control the process for stimulating this business activity, one does not control the results of these efforts.

It is imperative, therefore, that the work program and its projects and tasks be designed carefully so that they lead to the achievement of the goals and objectives of the local economic development program. The effective management of this work program requires an evaluation process that monitors progress, assesses the performance of the program and its projects, and measures the impact that this program is creating. If during the course of the evaluation it is determined that it is not meeting these goals and objectives with the strategies that have been adopted, and it is not reaching the level of impact needed or desired, then one must revise the program to make it more effective. That is the value of evaluation. It provides a systematic basis for assessing where one is in relation to where one wants to be. It also enables one to formulate timely decisions for the more effective use of valuable and limited resources. If the reporting system can only provide feedback considerably after the fact, as a matter of history, then the economic development director/project manager cannot control his or her economic development program.

PART 4

The Organizational Challenge

Organizing and Staffing Local Economic Development Programs

——————————— Robert R. Weaver

Local economic development programs in Texas are organized in a variety of ways. The form of each program has been determined primarily by the groups involved in its initiation and the political philosophies of these groups.

Organizational models

The structures of local economic development organizations in Texas can be classified into six models based on the way in which they were initiated, the community sector exercising primary control, and their modes of operation. All of these schemes have some potential for success, but those which represent genuine partnerships between public and private interests in the community are generally considered the most promising. These models, their basic characteristics, and some of their advantages and disadvantages are discussed below.

The public-assisted private model The traditional organization structure for local economic development, and the one still found in nearly half of all Texas cities, is the *public-assisted private model.* In this form a private organization (usually the chamber of commerce or one of its divisions) has primary responsibility for the program, and the city government provides financial support to the effort. Activities generally emphasize attempts to attract new business and industry to the area, and there is usually a convention and tourism component. Local government tends to be passive, becoming actively involved in the program only when asked to assist with spe-

Reprinted with permission from Robert R. Weaver, *Local Economic Development in Texas* (Arlington: Institute of Urban Studies, University of Texas, 1986).

cific project approvals or authorizations such as zoning or tax-exempt project financing. The advantage of such a program is that the private sector organization usually has more experience and expertise, at least in the limited activities which are commonly undertaken, than does the city government and is able to enhance its efforts through the public support provided. The disadvantage for the public sector is that its goals are not necessarily represented in the program, nor does it have the opportunity to target activities to special community problems which may arise.

The public proprietary model   During the 1960s many purely public economic development programs were established in Texas. Traditional federally funded urban renewal and its successor programs were operated by local governments with little or no involvement of the private sector. These programs emphasized clearance and redevelopment of blighted areas and improvement of development-supporting infrastructure. The concept behind these programs was the idea that government could cause private sector development to occur simply by preparing suitable development sites where none had existed before. This same idea led to the establishment of industrial parks in cities throughout the state, often with the assistance of the federal Economic Development Administration.

The premise behind these programs has largely been discredited by the poor results of many local efforts. It is now generally acknowledged that these programs are fatally flawed because they lack the necessary involvement of the private sector.

The private proprietary model   In some Texas cities economic development is almost entirely a function of the private sector. In these areas the local program is planned, funded, and implemented by private interests, often acting through a non-profit corporation or foundation. The organization usually does not seek local government financial assistance or other aid either in the development or implementation of its program.

These programs may target fairly small geographic areas and often have limited objectives. It is not unusual for such a program to exist in a city along with one or more of the other organizational types discussed in this chapter.

The disadvantage of this model is that it fails to tap the financial assistance and development incentives which local government can provide. The concurrent advantage, however, is that the private sector organization "owns" the program and, therefore, has full control of its activities. It also has the advantage of allowing the organization to make plans and conduct sensitive negotiations without the risk of premature public disclosure. One danger for the public sector is that programs organized in this way can easily be converted to the "private political model" discussed below.

The private political model   This organizational model is similar in many ways to the "private proprietary model," with the principal difference being in the implementation strategy used. Program planning is still done and financed by a private sector group, but once the program is developed, the organization becomes a political pressure group which attempts to gain local government adoption and financing of at least part of its program. The strategy often includes a concerted effort to get the local city council to authorize bond issues and apply for federal and state grants to fund projects, to enact changes in local development policies which would be beneficial to the organization's program, and to initiate local financial incentives such as tax abatement and tax increment financing. Sometimes the relationship between the organization and the city government is adversarial, but in other cases the private group is able to gain public support and local government endorsement of its program.

The private-initiated partnership model   Many of the more recently organized local economic development programs in Texas are a joint effort of the public and private sectors. Because in many cities the private sector has traditionally been more active in economic development than the city government, it becomes the primary initiator of the new program. The partnership develops as local government becomes more interested in taking an active role in economic development and the private sector sees this as an opportunity to gain public assistance and support for its efforts.

Sometimes a completely new organizational structure is formed, but often the city simply "buys in" to the existing private decision-making process. The city usually brings with it, however, an agenda which is somewhat different from that of the private sector. If this is so, a process for working out the differences will probably occur. The city may create a staff capacity to work with the private sector in this effort, and what often emerges is a hybrid program which includes elements from both sectors.

This marriage also introduces the problem of the city government's being required to justify public support of special-interest activities, and it may require that a general public interest be identified if such projects are to be included in the program. This is sometimes difficult and may be a serious disadvantage of the structure, but it may be outweighed by the advantages of merging resources from both sectors into a coordinated effort.

The public-initiated partnership model   Public-initiated partnerships usually develop in cities with histories of involvement in public proprietary efforts in which the private sector has not been especially active in economic development. The city may attempt to overcome the deficiencies of its previous efforts by bringing the pri-

vate sector into its program. This can be accomplished either by
establishment of a private sector policy body within the city government structure or by city-initiated formation of a new public/private
local organization, such as a Local Development Corporation.[1]

Usually the city government provides most of the funding for
the organization and retains control through the appropriations process. Sometimes the city goes to great lengths to make the organization appear independent of local government while retaining primary control. The weakness of such a structure is that unless the
private sector is an enthusiastic partner and is given a significant
role, the effort remains primarily public without the degree of private sector support needed to make it effective.

Choosing an organizational model

The choice of an organizational model for a local economic development program is a decision which should reflect the basic philosophies of the community's public and private sector leaders and rec-
ognize the history of past efforts. There are, however, several
criteria that city leaders should consider in selecting a structure
which will be most likely to meet the city government's needs.
These include the:

Degree of control the city government wishes to have over the organization and its activities

Amount of public funds the city is willing to invest in the effort

Appropriateness of the structure for working toward the specific
goals which have been set for the program.

Figure 1 characterizes each of the models in terms of the potential
degree of control they afford to the city government, the likely level
of public investment which will be required, and the goals for which
each is best suited.

It should also be noted that the city government will not have
the discretion to choose an organizational structure where private
political or private proprietary organizations are already in place,
unless it wishes to attempt to convert these to another model or to
establish a separate program. The establishment of one of these private-sector–dominated structures can result, however, in demands
being placed on city government which will significantly impact on
municipal operations, and cities must be prepared to respond effectively to these demands to protect the public interest.

Staffing local economic development programs

Once a city government decides to become actively involved in economic development it is immediately faced with the need to establish a staff capability to carry out the function. The level of staffing
required and its placement within the administrative structure of

Organizational type	Degree of city control	Public investment required	Appropriate goals
Public proprietary	Highest	Highest	Urban/slum clearance, infrastructure improvements, growth management, historic preservation
Public-initiated partnership	High	High	Urban/neighborhood redevelopment, mixed public/private projects, historic preservation, growth management
Private-initiated partnership	Moderate	Moderate	Downtown/commercial revitalization, tax increment/special assessment districts, tax-exempt financing, tax abatement
Private political	Low-moderate	Low-high	Tax-exempt financing, major community facilities, health & human service improvements
Public-assisted private	Low	Low-moderate	Convention/tourism, attracting new business/industry, expanding existing business/industry
Private proprietary	Lowest	Lowest	Targeted commercial development, retail/service growth, individual property improvement

Figure 1. Characteristics of local economic development organizational models.

the city is largely dictated by the way in which the local program has been organized and the amount of effort on the part of the city which will be required.

The *public-assisted private* structure, which is still the most common in Texas cities, and the *private-initiated partnership* model require minimal city staff effort. Where these have been implemented, however, it is usually desirable that the city staff contact be at a high level in the administration. In Texas cities the city manager is most likely to be the staff person responsible for economic development, and there may not be any additional staff assigned specifically to the function.

The *public proprietary* and the *public-initiated partnership* models require a high level of staff effort. Cities with these organizational forms usually create a separate department or division with a director and supporting staff positions.

Cities with a *private political* structure in place must have a strong staff capability in order to deal effectively with the demands placed on the city government by the private sector organization. The level and capability of city staffing should be equal to that of the private organization.

In cities where the only economic development structure in place is the *private proprietary* model there may be little need for the city to staff for economic development. The interface necessary between the city and the private group usually can be accomplished through normal channels and existing departments.

Organizational assignment of economic development   A survey by the International City Management Association in 1984 asked cities throughout the U.S. to report their assignment of the economic development function within their administrative structures, and the 1986 Institute of Urban Studies survey solicited similar information from Texas cities.[2] Results of both surveys are displayed in Table 1.

These results indicate that Texas cities are more likely to assign responsibility for economic development to the city manager's office than are U.S. cities in general. This is probably due to the significant number who said that the function is primarily performed in a non-city agency (such as the chamber of commerce) and who named the city manager as the city's contact with the agency.

The results also show that Texas cities are more likely to have established separate economic development departments within their staff structures, and that they are somewhat more likely to assign the function to a line department (the Institute survey found

Table 1. Organizational assignment of economic development in Texas and U.S. cities.

Organizational unit assigned economic development	Percentage of U.S. cities	Percentage of Texas cities
Office of city manager/CAO	28	44
Separate department	13	21
Line department	*28	33
Larger community and economic development agency	31	3

*Includes both decentralized and partially centralized assignment.

Table 2. Staff assignment of economic development in Texas cities.

Position title	Percentage of cities
City manager/CAO	38
Economic development director/coordinator/specialist	28
Director of planning/planner	25
Other	9

that the Planning Department was most often chosen). It is also apparent that Texas cities have not been active in establishing larger Community and Economic Development (CED) agencies.

Staff assignment of economic development   Texas cities have increasingly recognized the need to provide staffing for the economic development function, and more than one-third of those responding to the Institute of Urban Studies survey in 1986 reported that they had created a new staff position responsible for economic development within the past five years. While the city manager is still the staff position most often named by cities as having primary staff responsibility for economic development, over sixty percent identify some other position, and nearly half of these report a position with the title of Economic Development Director, Coordinator, or Specialist. Table 2 lists the staff position with primary responsibility for economic development as reported by Texas cities in the Institute survey.

Education and experience of economic development staff   The education and experience of persons occupying municipal economic development staff positions in Texas reflect both the relatively short history of municipal involvement in the function and the lack of opportunities for formal education in the field. The Institute survey reported that persons filling the staff position designated as having primary economic development responsibility most often have academic degrees and training in public administration (41%) because so many city managers are designated, and planning degrees (28%) because planning is the department to which the function is most often assigned.

These individuals have experience almost exclusively in municipal government in Texas. Two-thirds have served in a similar position in another city in the state, and less than ten percent have private sector experience. Only one-sixth have experience outside Texas, and over a quarter report no prior economic development experience at all.

When we look only at the persons filling city staff positions with

Table 3. *Economic development assistance received by Texas cities* (appended from Chapter 4 of Robert R. Weaver, *Local Economic Development in Texas* [Arlington: Institute of Urban Studies, University of Texas, 1986]).

Source	Percentage of cities receiving assistance
Federal agencies	
Department of Housing & Urban Development	36
Economic Development Administration	33
International Trade Commission	5
Federal Aviation Administration	3
State agencies	
Texas Economic Development Commission	79
Governor's Office of Economic Development	44
Texas Department of Community Affairs	36
Texas Historical Commission	31
Texas Housing Agency	13
Texas Advisory Commission on Intergovernmental Relations	3
Texas Employment Commission	3
Regional agencies	
Councils of governments/Economic development districts	44
Municipal organizations	
International City Management Association	41
Texas Municipal League	38
National League of Cities	21
Public Technology, Inc.	3
Other membership organizations	
Urban Land Institute	10
International Downtown Executives Association	8
American Institute of Architects	8
American Institute of Certified Planners	3
American Economic Development Council	3
Council of Urban Economic Development	3
Other sources	
Private consultants	38
Colleges and universities	21

the title of Economic Development Director, Coordinator, or Specialist, a somewhat different picture emerges. Two-thirds of these persons have academic training in either business or economics. It appears that when Texas cities create a professional economic development staff position, they usually fill it with a person whose academic background is oriented more toward private business and economics than to public administration and planning. Still, only about one-third of these professionals report having prior private or non-profit economic development experience, and only about one in five have experience outside the state.

When asked about the need for educational opportunities in the field of economic development, cities are almost unanimous in their opinion that economic development should be included in the curricula of public administration programs in the state and that Texas colleges and universities should offer degrees or major concentrations in economic development.

1. For a full description of local development corporations see: *Local Development Corporation: A Tool for Economic Development,* International City Management Associa-

tion, MIS Report, Vol. 17, No. 4, June, 1985.

2. *Facilitating Economic Development,* Baseline Data Report 16, no. 11/12 (1984): 3.

Evaluating Nonfinancial Business Assistance Programs

Harry P. Hatry, Mark Fall,
Thomas O. Singer, and E. Blaine Liner

Editor's note: Although the procedures described in this article were developed for economic development programs at the state level, many of the recommendations are appropriate to the local level as well. In addition, the evaluation of nonfinancial business assistance programs is but one example of detailed monitoring techniques that can be applied to a number of other aspects of economic development efforts, including business attraction, export promotion, tourism, and community development.

Scope

Many state and local governments provide technical assistance to businesses to help them function more effectively. Technical assistance can include seminars on regulations or other governance issues; individual counseling on business plans, marketing strategies, and financial plans; and referral to other sources of assistance, often to financial assistance programs. Technical assistance programs may also provide services to individuals (such as attorneys and accountants) who, in turn, use the information to help their clients.

These programs frequently are focused on small businesses or firms in particular markets, such as high-technology manufacturers, telecommunications firms, or biotechnology firms that the agency feels need assistance to compete in the marketplace. Programs also

Reprinted with permission from Harry P. Hatry, Mark Fall, Thomas O. Singer, and E. Blaine Liner, *Monitoring the Outcomes of Economic Development Programs* (Washington, D.C.: The Urban Institute Press, 1990), pp. 31–47. The section of the book reproduced here was originally entitled "Business Assistance (Nonfinancial) Programs."

may target firms that are in emerging markets to help them gain an advantage over competitors in other jurisdictions. Occasionally, special programs are designed to provide assistance to women and to minority-owned businesses.

The objectives of business assistance programs generally are to: (1) help improve business operations and their viability; (2) help firms comply with state regulations that govern their operations; (3) refer firms to other programs, such as financial assistance or export promotion programs, and other sources of technical assistance to help them improve or expand operations; and (4) help persons wanting to launch a business make good startup decisions. The long-term objectives of these programs include providing assistance that will help firms initiate operations, stay in business, increase sales, and expand their employment.

Performance indicators for business assistance programs

Exhibit 1 presents a set of performance indicators that can be used for monitoring business assistance programs. These are grouped into three categories: indicators of service quality, intermediate outcome indicators, and long-term outcome indicators. The information generated for these performance indicators comes from agency records, surveys of business assistance clients, and in some instances, from the state unemployment insurance (UI) database. A sample questionnaire is included at the end of this article as Exhibit 2.

Indicators of service quality Indicators of service quality can highlight specific aspects of service quality that need attention and improvement.

The *accuracy of information* (PI–1) provided to clients is particularly important for a technical assistance program. Firms come to the business assistance office for its expertise in an area, such as state regulation, and expect to receive accurate answers to their questions. Since the program's primary commodity is information, its accuracy, as found by the program's clients, is an important indicator of program performance.

Clients' perceptions of the *timeliness* (PI–2) of the services indicate the program's success in responding quickly to requests.

Some clients may not actually receive the services they sought from the program. The indicator showing the percentage who actually received the services they requested (PI–3) provides information on the actual receipt of desired services as perceived by clients. This indicator captures information that would be lost if the agency only sought information on the quality of services *received*, regardless of what was requested.

Ratings by clients of the *overall quality of the program's assist-*

ance (PI–4) provide the program with a composite rating for service quality. This indicator in effect combines into one rating the client's perspective on receipt of services, accuracy, timeliness, plus any other factors the client feels were important. The percentage of clients that indicate that they would recommend the program's services to other businesses (PI–5) is an indicator of overall client satisfaction and of the value of services. It has additional importance because clients often are a major source of program referrals. If clients are not satisfied with the assistance they receive, they are unlikely to recommend the services to others, thus decreasing the coverage of the program and possibly undermining long-term support for it.

Accuracy, timeliness, and overall quality should be queried for each individual service offered by the program, as illustrated in question 2 of the sample questionnaire (Exhibit 2). The questionnaire provides the opportunity to break out information on basic assistance services such as: publications, seminars and workshops, counseling, and referrals. This list can be modified to meet any agency's particular variety of business assistance programs.

Publications are usually the primary information tool provided to clients. Indeed, publications are often the only contact the program has with a client. Seminars or workshops are given on general or specific topics of interest to businesses. They may be attended by owners or employees of businesses, or by those who will use the information to assist their own clients to improve their businesses. Ratings of seminars and workshops provide the program with information on the quality of these activities. Individual counseling is a one-on-one service for businesses on specific issues, such as development of a business plan, a marketing strategy, or an operational problem. Ratings of this service provide information from those clients who received the in-person assistance. Referrals to other sources of assistance, whether a different department, a different level of government, or a private source, are a significant service if the program has limited technical services of its own or is not the appropriate source for certain types of assistance or information. Ratings of this service can help the program judge whether its referrals have been useful.

The survey questionnaire should ask respondents to give their reasons for poor ratings. The business assistance program can obtain valuable information from these reasons. As illustrated by questions 2f and 3a of Exhibit 2, the questionnaire requests respondents to explain any poor ratings. Such information should be compiled and subsequently analyzed by program staff to provide clues to problems with the program and how they might be corrected.

Intermediate outcome indicators   Intermediate outcome indicators are indicators that, although not measuring increased employment or sales, nevertheless represent actions taken by clients that can be considered important, positive steps toward these desired outcomes.

The percentage of clients that decided to start a business is an important intermediate outcome indicator for programs that provide technical assistance to start businesses (PI-6a). However, the list of indicators (Exhibit 1) does not include businesses that decide to defer or abandon forming a new business. Although the program's assistance may alert the clients about serious competitive weaknesses that result in postponement or abandonment of start-ups, such situations are likely to be secondary to the program's objectives and have not been included as a major performance indicator (although such data can be sought, as shown in question 4 of Exhibit 2). This information can be reported as individual outcome indicators or as one summary indicator, as shown in Exhibit 1.

Another important intermediate outcome for clients is alteration of their business or market strategy, based on the service (PI-6b)—for example, a shift to a new product or market segment. Such outcomes indicate that the firm is adopting new long-term strategies to improve performance.

Solving operational problems (e.g., obtaining permits) or improving regular business operations or methods (e.g., working capital management) are also relevant outcomes (PI-6c and d). These outcomes tend to strengthen the firm's ability to stay in business and grow.

Only asking clients whether such outcomes occurred does not tell whether the business assistance program had any role in these outcomes. To address this issue, clients should also be queried about the extent to which the program's assistance contributed to these outcomes (question 5 of Exhibit 2). To calculate the values for PI-6, therefore, the agency will need to combine (1) information from each client as to whether the intermediate outcomes occurred with (2) the same client's rating of the extent of the business assistance program's contribution. This should be accomplished in the data processing step. The agency can also tabulate the answers to the question on the extent of contribution without directly linking the contribution to the specific outcome categories—as an added intermediate outcome indicator.

To what extent will respondents be able to answer accurately about the business assistance program's contribution to outcomes? This is a major technical issue for these procedures. The answer depends on the extent to which the respondent knows about, and can recall accurately, circumstances regarding the program's assistance and subsequent actions by the respondent's firm. Although 100 percent accuracy in the responses to these questions cannot be expected, asking key representatives of client firms for their perceptions appears to be the only practical way to obtain at least rough information on the extent of contribution. Note that while the *precision* of the indicators is in considerable doubt, they should be *accurate* enough to identify major differences over time and across different types of businesses.

End (long-term) outcomes End (long-term) outcome indicators (PI–7 and 8) assess the extent to which the business assistance program helped firms increase their sales and employment. These are generally the major long-term objectives of business assistance programs. PI–7, percentage of clients who actually start businesses or expand them and increase jobs and sales, is one of the long-term outcomes of a business assistance program. Jobs added by those actually starting or expanding a business, PI–8, is another, perhaps the single most important, outcome.

As with the intermediate outcomes, an indication by a firm that these results have occurred does not tell whether the program helped to bring them about. *The contribution of the service received by clients to end outcomes realized is a central concern of performance monitoring.* Only in instances where clients indicated that the services they received contributed to the outcomes they experienced can the program really take credit for these outcomes. As with the intermediate outcomes, the most practical way to obtain this information appears to be to ask clients about the extent of the business assistance program's contribution, as illustrated in question 5 of Exhibit 2. Issues and cautions regarding this procedure were discussed previously under "Intermediate Outcome Indicators."

The *number* of new jobs, PI–8, poses additional concerns about accuracy. Asking respondents for exact numbers is likely to create considerable difficulties for many respondents. To ease their burden and encourage responses to the question, clients might better be asked to check off ranges of results (0–4, 5–9, etc.). This procedure is illustrated in question 4l of Exhibit 2. An alternative procedure is to track changes in employment for clients through the state's UI database. This procedure should give reasonably accurate estimates of employment levels for each month. UI data will not, however, by themselves provide information as to the contribution of the program to the increases in jobs.

The matter of when to survey clients is an important issue. Clients should be surveyed approximately nine months to one year after they begin receiving services. This time interval balances potential client memory problems on the one hand with, on the other hand, the need to allow sufficient time to elapse for significant outcomes to occur.

Disaggregations of indicator data
The performance indicator values should be broken out by key characteristics of the client firms, to make the indicators most useful to

program managers. The disaggregations for these programs should include: (1) size of firm (as measured by number of employees); (2) standard industrial classification (SIC) code (two-digit codes should be sufficient—if the program focuses on a particular set of industries, the data should be presented for these industries); (3) area (county)—perhaps arranged to distinguish urban from rural areas; and, possibly, (4) minority status.

Firm size is important, particularly for programs that target small- and medium-sized firms. This breakout will show program differences in service to firms of different sizes. The industry category breakout will show how well the program is serving different industries in the state. It will be especially helpful if the program is targeting certain industries for assistance. Area disaggregations should allow the program to gauge how it is doing with firms in different parts of the jurisdiction. For state agencies, these regions could be aggregations of counties that the program finds to be similar, perhaps because of certain shared characteristics, or because these are the economic development regions used for other agency purposes. These counties can be grouped into regions based on geographic contiguity, although they could be based on other factors, such as metropolitan or nonmetropolitan. The minority status breakout will provide information on the program's success in reaching minority firms.

Sources for performance data

Program records   Information from program records is needed to: (1) provide basic client information in order to contact clients with a survey questionnaire or to track employment through the UI database such as firm name, address, name and title of key contact person, telephone number, dates of service provided, and the firm's federal or state identification number (for determining a firm's growth in employment); and (2) obtain information on client characteristics needed for disaggregating performance indicators, such as firm size, industry, region, information about the services each client received, and minority status. The program's database on its clients should contain information on each firm that receives assistance. The program can obtain this information from each firm as part of its regular client information system at the time clients first seek assistance.

Client surveys   Client surveys provide the major source of information on program quality and outcomes. Surveys generate data on clients' perception of service quality, on the outcomes they have experienced, and on the contribution of the program's services to the outcomes.

The program should consider surveying on a quarterly basis all those who received assistance from the program. If the number of quarterly clients is large, say over 200, and the data collection costs are a problem, the agency can survey a sample of clients in a manner to ensure that the findings are representative. The sample might be a random selection of all clients, or a stratified sample to achieve representation of all clients on different services received, size groups, industries, and location within the jurisdiction in order to later break out the performance data.

For performance monitoring purposes, the program should define reasonably precisely who is a client. To avoid excessive cost and little extra value, it should establish the amount of a service that needs to be provided for a firm to be classified as a client. For example, it might specify that the firm needs to receive a minimum of four hours of assistance before being categorized as a client. This amount could vary for each type of service. A firm requesting one business assistance program publication, for example, should not be included in the client survey.

Clients can be surveyed approximately nine months to one year after receiving assistance. If the survey is earlier, such as after three months, not enough time will have elapsed for many clients to have achieved long-term, or even intermediate outcomes. By the same token, if the survey is delayed much later, to more than one year, the individuals in the firms will likely have major problems remembering the assistance given them and/or the outcomes relating to the assistance. Also, at this later date, the relevance of the performance information is likely to lessen because of staff, program, and funding changes.

For each client to be surveyed, probably by mail, the program needs to provide the names of the primary contact persons, their address, and telephone number (for telephone reminders to firms not returning questionnaires). To disaggregate the survey data, the program should also collect and provide the SIC, size, location (county), and minority status of the firm.

The survey questionnaire should include questions on the quality of the services received, the outcomes experienced, and clients' estimation of the contribution of the services to these outcomes. Exhibit 2 illustrates how this can be done. A few open-ended questions should be included so that respondents can give reasons why they answered in certain ways, especially if they report poor ratings. (See, for example, questions 2f, 5a, and 7a in Exhibit 2.) Open-ended questions can also be included to ask for suggestions to improve the program's services. (See, for example, question 9 in Exhibit 2.)

Mailed questionnaires should be sent with a personalized cover letter signed by a top executive such as the government's chief executive or agency head. The letter should indicate the need for feedback to improve the program's services and should point out that information will be kept confidential and only reported in aggregate form. An incentive to respond is desirable. As an incentive to respond, an attractive professional publication or a report could be offered to those who return the questionnaires.

State unemployment insurance data   The state UI database can be used to determine the change in employment of assisted firms. Program personnel should be asked to request the identification number from clients as part of one of the initial contacts. (The UI database contains federal and state identification numbers for each firm that pays taxes on employees in the state.) If the program does not obtain an identification number, it may still be possible to find the firm in the UI database by using the firm's name and county code. Because of certain characteristics in the system, it may not be possible to find all firms using the company name and county code.

The UI database can be used to track the monthly employment of assisted firms. The system collects monthly employment figures from firms on a quarterly basis. The program could identify employment change in assisted firms for several quarters. The UI data are useful because they allow the program to track long-term outcomes over a longer time period than can be obtained from a client survey.

Although this procedure is attractive, it has two important limitations. It can obtain quite accurate employment figures, but these will not tell whether the business assistance program contributed directly to increases in employment. Nor does the system provide information on service quality, as does the client survey procedure. Thus, the UI database should preferably be considered as a complement to client survey procedures, especially for providing data on the amount of job growth for use in PI–8.

Explanatory data

The program may want to provide explanatory data along with the performance indicator information, to help explain major improvements, or declines, in program performance. For example, various national, state, or local economic indicators are likely to be relevant, since the intermediate and long-term indicators can be affected by economic conditions. The rate of economic growth for the jurisdiction is one indicator of the general economic climate. If the jurisdiction's growth rate slows or increases rapidly, the outcomes of firms receiving assistance would, in general, be expected to also reflect these conditions. Significant external events such as changes in competition from other countries can also affect outcomes for firms in specific industries.

Reporting the results

A major need in performance monitoring is for results to be presented to program and other agency managers in clear, informative formats. Exhibits 3 and 4 present two examples. Exhibit 3 illustrates a format designed to show the detailed findings on each specific performance indicator, with breakouts by major client characteristics. The user can quickly identify those categories of clients for whom performance on the indicator was particularly high or low during the period covered by the report. Exhibit 4 shows a *summary* report format, presenting data for each performance indicator that compare current performance to prior performance and to targets set by the program.

Exhibit 1. Performance indicators for business assistance programs.

Service quality indicators

PI–1   Percentage of clients rating the *accuracy of information* for each service received as excellent or good (question 2, Exhibit 2).

PI–2   Percentage of clients rating the *timeliness* of the services received as excellent or good (question 2, Exhibit 2).

PI–3   Percentage of clients reporting that they received the services they requested (question 3, Exhibit 2).

PI–4   Percentage of clients rating the *overall quality* of assistance of each service as excellent or good (question 2, Exhibit 2).

PI–5   Percentage of clients who would recommend program assistance to other businesses (question 7, Exhibit 2).

Intermediate outcome indicators

PI–6   Number and percentage of clients that (a) decided to start a business; (b) made a significant change in the nature of their business or markets; (c) solved an operational problem; or (d) improved regular business operations or methods; *and,* if any of these occurred, also reported that the business assistance program office's assistance contributed at least somewhat to the outcome (questions 4a, 4f, 4g, 4h, and 5, Exhibit 2).

End (long-term) outcome indicators

PI–7   Number and percentage of clients that (a) actually started a business; (b) expanded current operations; (c) increased sales; or (d) increased the number of employees; *and,* if any of these occurred, also reported that the business assistance program contributed at least somewhat to the outcomes (questions 4c, 4d, 4i, 4j, and 5, Exhibit 2).

PI–8   Number of additional jobs, as reported by clients (question 4l, Exhibit 2) *and* for which clients reported that the business assistance program contributed at least somewhat to the outcome—or the number of additional jobs indicated by state unemployment insurance data (questions 4l and 5 of Exhibit 2— or unemployment insurance data).

Note: The information in parentheses refers to the source of data for each indicator.

Exhibit 2. Sample client questionnaire for business assistance programs.

1. For what purpose did you seek assistance in the past 12 months from the Business Assistance Office? (PLEASE CIRCLE.)

		Yes	No
a.	Business startup help...............................	1	2
b.	Expansion of existing business	1	2
c.	Technical assistance on a specific problem..........	1	2
d.	Questions or problems with licensing or government relations.............................	1	2
e.	Other (please specify)	1	2

2. Please rate the following characteristics for the services you received from the Business Assistance Program. (PLEASE CIRCLE.)

    Rating scale: 1 = excellent; 2 = good; 3 = fair; 4 = poor.

Service received	Did not request the service	Accuracy of information	Timeliness	Overall quality of assistance
a. Publications	N	1 2 3 4	1 2 3 4	1 2 3 4
b. Seminars/ workshops	N	1 2 3 4	1 2 3 4	1 2 3 4
c. Counseling	N	1 2 3 4	1 2 3 4	1 2 3 4
d. Referrals	N	1 2 3 4	1 2 3 4	1 2 3 4
e. Other (specify):	N	1 2 3 4	1 2 3 4	1 2 3 4

    f. If you rated any of the characteristics in Question 2 as Fair or Poor, please explain why.

3. Did you get the services you requested? (PLEASE CIRCLE ONE.)

    Yes   1
    No   2

    a. If no, would you please explain what you wanted but did not get?

4. Since the time you began receiving assistance from the Business Assistance Program have you: (PLEASE CIRCLE ALL THAT APPLY.)

		Yes	No
a.	Decided to go into business........................	1	2
b.	Decided not to go into business	1	2
c.	Actually started a business	1	2
d.	Expanded current operations.......................	1	2
e.	Decided not to expand.............................	1	2
f.	Made a significant change in the nature of your business or in your markets	1	2
g.	Solved a specific operational problem	1	2
h.	Improved regular business operations or methods	1	2
i.	Increased your sales...............................	1	2
j.	Increased the number of employees................	1	2

k. Gone out of business.............................   1   2

l. If you indicated that you had actually started a business (4c) or increased your employment (4j), please indicate the approximate number of additional full-time equivalent employees: (PLEASE CIRCLE ONE.)

1–4	1
5–9	2
10–19	3
20 or more	4

5. To what extent do you feel that the services you received from the Business Assistance Program contributed to the outcomes identified in Question 4? (PLEASE CIRCLE ONE.)

Contributed significantly	1
Contributed somewhat	2
Did not contribute to the outcome	3
Service detracted	4
Don't know	5

a. If in Question 5 you answered that the service did not contribute to the outcome or detracted from it, please explain why.

6. How did you hear about the assistance you received from the Business Assistance Program? (PLEASE CIRCLE THE SINGLE MOST IMPORTANT SOURCE.)

Media advertising	1
Referral by a Small Business Development Center (SBDC)	2
Referral by another government agency	3
Referral by a private business adviser (such as attorneys or accountants)	4
Referral by a bank or lending institution	5
A Business Asssistance Office publication	6
Other publications	7
Word of mouth (e.g., business acquaintance)	8

7. Would you recommend that other small businesses contact the Business Assistance Program for help? (PLEASE CIRCLE.)

Yes	1
No	2

a. If No, would you please explain why not?

8. How available is information on the services of the state's Business Assistance Program in your community? (PLEASE CIRCLE.)

Very available	1
Somewhat available	2
Only a little	3
Not at all	4

9. Do you have any other comments or suggestions that would help the Business Assistance Program improve its services to businesses?

Thank you for your help!

Exhibit 3. Example of a detailed report format for business assistance programs.

Performance indicator PI–4: Percentage of clients who rated the overall quality of referrals as excellent, good, fair, or poor.

	Number in sample	Percentage			
		Excellent	Good	Fair	Poor
Total					
Size (*Number of employees*)					
1–9					
10–19					
20–99					
100–499					
500 and up					
Industry sector					
20					
30					
40					
50					
60					
Region					
Region 1					
Region 2					
Region 3					
Region 4					
Minority status					
Black					
Female					
Hispanic					
Asian					
Other					

Exhibit 4. Example of summary report format for business assistance programs.

Performance indicators	Most recent period	Last period	Year to date	Year to date last year	Target % for current year
Service quality indicators					
PI–1 Percentage of clients who rated the accuracy of information for all services as excellent or good					
PI–2 Percentage of clients who rated the timeliness of all services as excellent or good					
PI–3 Percentage of clients reporting that they received the service requested					
PI–4 Percentage of clients who rated the overall quality of all services as excellent 34good					
PI–5 Percentage of clients who recommended program services to other businesses					

Performance indicators	Most recent period	Last period	Year to date	Year to date last year	Target % for current year
Intermediate outcome indicators PI–6 Percentage of clients who (a) decided to start a business; (b) made a significant change in the nature of their business or markets; (c) solved an operational problem; or (d) improved regular business operations or methods; *and* reported that the business assistance office's programs contributed at least somewhat to the outcome.					
Long-term outcome indicators PI–7 Number and percentage of clients that (a) actually started a business: (b) expanded current operations; (c) increased sales; or (d) increased the number of employees—*and* reported that the business assistance program contributed at least somewhat to the outcomes.					
PI–8 Number of additional jobs for which clients reported that the business assistance program contributed at least somewhat to the outcome.					

The Emerging Third Wave: New Economic Development Strategies

————————— Doug Ross and Robert E. Friedman

Today state and local elected officials and economic development professionals find themselves in an increasingly difficult bind. On one hand, federal and state budget problems are choking off the public resources available for economic development activities. On the other hand, poll after poll shows that voters hold elected officials, especially their governors, responsible for the performance of their local economies.

Fortunately, state and local economic developers across the country are in the process of inventing a new generation of development strategies that respond to these conflicting demands. These policies offer a way out: more economic impact for the public dollar. They are the emerging "Third Wave" of public economic development practice in the past half-century.

To understand this latest wave of change, still gathering force and only recently visible, it is helpful to put it in context, to examine the imprints left in the wake of its two preceding waves, and to see the broader revolution that has been changing the rules of the economic development game.

The rise and fall of the First Wave

Until a decade ago, most state economic development strategies had a single focus: recruit new plants from outside the state. How? Offer them low-cost investment locations and public financial incentives.

Reprinted by permission of the Corporation For Enterprise Development (CFED) from *Entrepreneurial Economy Review* (Autumn 1990): 3–10. Mitchell Horowitz and Janet Topolsky contributed substantially to this article. CFED, 777 North Capitol St., N.E., #801, Washington, D. C. 20002.

Chasing the almighty smokestack Born in the South in hopes of luring manufacturing branch plants from the North with offers of cheap, non-union labor, cut-rate land prices and low taxes, this industrial recruitment or "smokestack chasing" strategy worked well for quite awhile. During the 1950s and 1960s, adherents in the South experienced dramatic employment and wage increases relative to the rest of the country. As northeastern and midwestern industrial states began to feel the impact of these aggressive assaults on their manufacturing firms, they fought back with First Wave policies of their own. States from one corner of America to another enacted their own arrays of expensive tax abatements, new job tax credits, training programs, low-interest loans and other government subsidies to lower the cost of doing business. In virtually every state, doing "economic development" meant organizing an industrial sales force in the state's economic development agency, arming it with a menu of subsidies to lure footloose plants and back-office operations across state lines.

The reason First Wave development policies worked from the '50s to the '70s, especially in poor states, was because at that point corporations were seeking the cheapest locations for branch plant operations that relied primarily on the use of unskilled labor. Moreover, most firms limited their searches to the continental United States.

However, by the late '70s and early '80s, evidence was growing that First Wave policies were losing their effectiveness. The South's success at closing its income gap with the rest of the country crested in 1976, after which the gap started growing again. Textile mills lured from New England to the Carolinas a decade earlier collapsed or fled off-shore to cheaper venues in record numbers. Manufacturing states like Michigan, Pennsylvania and Ohio found that, after the 1980–82 recession, smokestack chasing no longer provided a means to generate enough new jobs or overcome problems in their traditional industries—automobiles, steel, machine tools, rubber—which were losing both U.S. market share and jobs.

The forces of change What happened? Two separate but related forces undermined First Wave policies.

The economy went global First, America was forced to participate more fully in the international economy. National boundaries became much less important in economic decisions. Whereas in 1960, only 20% of U.S.-produced goods faced foreign competition, by 1980 more than 70% were fighting off international competitors. Dramatic decreases in transportation and communication costs made it easier to ship existing production technologies to wherever the cheapest available workforce lived. Companies looking for cheap, unskilled labor and low-cost locations were no longer confined to the

U.S. As inexpensive as rural Mississippi or some Sunbelt locale might be, Mexico was cheaper, and Sri Lanka cheaper yet. No matter how large their incentives or low their wages and taxes, U.S. communities could no longer compete as the lowest-cost location for production.

Technology got sophisticated   Even while Third World nations were threatening U.S. markets with bargain goods, some developed-world European and Asian competitors were challenging us with higher quality goods. In some cases, better organized people or production processes produced the higher quality. But in many other countries—especially Japan and Germany—better product development was also related to the sophisticated use of new computer-based information technologies. As more and more firms in Asia, Europe and the U.S. were demonstrating, you could still lead in goods and service production in the face of Third World low-wage competition. But to do so required the ability to customize previously mass-produced products with better quality to satisfy niche markets. This, in turn, generated a growing demand for more educated workers and higher technology capabilities. These resources were not central to most First Wave strategies.

But cost isn't everything   Along with these changes, states also began to focus on where their jobs were coming from. New studies revealed that recruitment ranked a distant third as a source of new jobs. Instead, existing firm expansions and start-up businesses were creating 80–90% of new jobs in most states. At best, recruited companies were producing the 10–20% remaining—and in many states with aggressive recruitment policies, it had fallen to less than 10%. Indeed, MIT researcher David Birch, in his pivotal paper "The Job Generation Process," documented that growth-oriented small businesses—not the target of recruitment efforts—were the leading source of job creation in the U.S. His finding was verified by the Brookings Institution and the Small Business Administration, among others.

As governors consulted with state business leaders about how to respond to these new forces, they began to hear a new set of concerns. They heard that key economic competitors—Japan and West Germany, in particular—were now beating the U.S. not by virtue of low cost. They were beating domestic firms on dimensions that were increasingly important in international competition: workforce quality; access to technology; and capital availability for modernization, new product development, market intelligence, and other opportunities.

Gradually, state policy makers realized a new economic truth. It was no longer enough for U.S. enterprise to be free, though that was still essential. It now also had to be competitive. Case in point:

it had not mattered twenty years earlier if 20% of General Motors' workers were functionally illiterate—because 20% of Ford's and Chrysler's couldn't read either. But when Japan emerged as a major competitor, and 100% of the Toyota City workers could read, U.S. firms found themselves at an important competitive disadvantage.

The Second Wave is born

As the 1980s unfolded, a "Second Wave" of economic development policy began to take shape. What changed was focus: development practitioners no longer gazed outside state borders; they concentrated on "homegrown" or indigenous economic development activity. States began to realize that to help their existing firms and attract new investment, the production inputs in the local economy— a skilled workforce, risk capital, available technology, sophisticated management information and modern telecommunications—would have to be world-competitive in quality and cost. State government's new role was to ensure that their resources or "competitive capacities" were available.

A new consciousness   States began fashioning a rich variety of experiments in Second Wave capacity-building. Dozens of states launched public programs to close the capital gaps discovered in state financial markets, modernize small- and medium-sized manufacturing firms, accelerate the development and transfer of new technologies from university to business, improve worker skills, equip entrepreneurs with management information to support higher rates of new business formation and growth, and actively encourage exporting.

Indeed, as the 1980s closed, a Second Wave action consensus had crystallized in America's state capitals. David Osborne, in his influential *Laboratories of Democracy*, noted that during the 1980s states had established over 100 public investment funds and over 25 public venture-capital funds, and launched over 200 programs to stimulate technological innovation. The Corporation for Enterprise Development's *1990 Development Report Card for the States* showed those figures increasing and further documented that 47 states had undertaken specific education reform measures, as well as efforts to improve the quality and productivity of their workforces. Indeed, the National Association of State Development Agencies, when it surveyed the states about development expenditures in 1988, found that roughly two-thirds of the states reporting allocated more budget resources to strengthening in-state businesses than to attracting outside businesses.

Homegrown enterprise   It's not that Second Wave adherents have abandoned industrial recruitment. They still market themselves aggressively to outside investors. But they do so knowing that footloose plants will produce only a marginal number of new jobs. And they recruit with the knowledge that cost is no longer the strongest magnet for new investment—rather it is an economic environment rich with the human, technological, financial and infrastructure resources that support existing firms and entrepreneurship.

The achievements of this quiet Second Wave revolution are significant. In state after state hit by ongoing industrial restructuring, the states that have cultivated homegrown enterprise and made long-term investments in their underlying competitive capacities have been able to come back from industrial shocks. Second Wave public policies appear to have contributed something to these recoveries.

The Second Wave Crests

The new concern: Impact Responsible state officials, strongly convinced that the dramatic shift to Second Wave policies has given state economic development efforts the right focus, feel growing apprehension about whether state agencies can perform Second Wave tasks *well*. In state after state, policymakers privately concede that the real impact of Second Wave programs seems to be considerably less than the sum of their parts. Marginal improvements in the right direction can be cited over and over again. But too often results do not seem transformational enough to reposition state and local economies to meet the global competition. In short, more and more leaders are questioning whether the programs they have initiated are *making a big enough difference*.

And so debate is shifting—from *what* needs to be done, where the consensus about indigenous development and "capacity-building" is quite firm, to *how to do it effectively*.

The Second Wave has limits, too In fact, even as capacity-building policies establish a positive record, four serious limitations that restrict their impact are emerging.

Scale is lacking Most state indigenous development efforts lack the scale needed if local business practice is to attain global standards. For example, most states, recognizing that seed and venture capital are critical to the creation of new firms and the development of new products, have created special funds to fill gaps in the availability of venture and seed capital. Yet, for the most part, these funds rarely exceed $5–10 million. Compared to the hundreds of millions of dollars a state's businesses may need in any given year, the funds are a drop in the bucket.

Similarly, state efforts to improve workforce skills typically center on short-term training for a few thousand people a year. Yet workforce experts predict that every American worker will need retraining at least once or twice during his career, with continual skill upgrading. Second Wave programs pale by comparison to the broad worker-training system the experts imply is needed to stay competitive.

Of course, providing for only a small fraction of the actual need in such capacity-building activities would be acceptable, even desirable, if programs encouraged others to supply the remaining service shortages. But such incentives are usually not included.

Service is fragmented   The Second Wave, zealous in covering every capacity need, wants for an important component of effective service. Second Wave effort is fractured, according to those capacity needs, with a separate program addressing each one. One program helps train workers, but is out of touch with the latest technology applications. Another helps identify practical ways to apply new technologies, but disclaims any knowledge or responsibility for capital availability to finance new equipment. Indeed, the proliferation of narrowly-focused development programs has created the appearance of significant activity, with little tangible result. Effective service delivery integrates resources and opportunities in ways that make them most useful to—and, therefore, most likely to be used by—customers.

Calls to overcome this chronic lack of program integration through "coordination" have been numerous. But the cabinet councils and other inter-agency groups created to handle the problem have yielded little but "turf" wars. Coordination, to paraphrase Sar Levitan, remains a unnatural act between two nonconsenting adults.

Programs lack accountability   Second Wave programs typically are not accountable to their customers. Few states, if any, accurately measure the performance of individual programs, much less their collective performance. So it is difficult to tell what has worked, or to learn from what has not.

Indeed, program survival is only loosely connected to customer satisfaction. Operating in effect as public monopolies, economic development programs are deprived of the automatic market feedback that signals success or failure in the private sector. Widespread refusal to use a particular government service—the way private market customers would signal dissatisfaction—is often not even visible to program staff. There is often no direct link between the program's customers and its managers. In fact, the primary market relationship is political, between program managers and the legislature. Lacking automatic measures of market acceptance, evaluation depends on the willingness of an incumbent administration to subject its own programs to independent scrutiny, an exercise most political leaders anticipating re-election would just as soon forego.

A link is missing   Second Wave strategies still short-shrift the link
between economic and social concerns. Established economic development approaches generally embody the perspective that all boats
will be lifted by a rising economic tide. They often do not meet the
people most in need. The 1980s proved that social and economic in-
equalities can grow during periods of economic expansion. Separat-
ing social issues from the economic development agenda only serves
to exacerbate the situation.

A deficient public technology   The First and Second Waves, it
turns out, do have something in common. As states have directed
their effort into building capacity rather than recruiting plants, they
have done so using the traditional First Wave public technology. If
they discover a capacity need or shortage—inadequate business
capital, a skill shortage, scarce entrepreneurship counseling—state
governments do what they have always done to produce change.
They create a program.

More often than not, it's a direct supplier program, one that
produces or procures the needed good or service and then provides
it directly to the customer. Launched with legislative authorization
and an annual legislative appropriation, such programs organize a
group of capable civil servants to operate as direct suppliers of the
good or service in short supply. A finance authority is established to
make direct loans to deserving businesses. Offices are opened where
civil servants dispense management information to entrepreneurs
seeking guidance. A local vocational education school or community
college is hired to offer training in some skill area deemed in short
supply.

The direct supplier program approach was adequate for the
First Wave. After all, industrial recruitment efforts usually targeted no more than several hundred businesses at any given time.
But, by contrast, Second Wave capacity-building aims at providing
thousands of businesses and several million citizens with the competitive resources they require.

Certainly, the responsibility for the impact deficiencies described above can be traced, in part, to the direct supplier nature of
the reigning public technology. When it comes to scale, such programs typically aspire to obtain a large enough public appropriation
to fill the entire resource gap—an ambition that is almost always
frustrated by limited public resources and competition from other
programs in the legislative process. Unlike private markets where
expanding customer demand usually brings forth private capital
streams to create enough supply, public sector capital decisions are
necessarily controlled by political and financial constraints, as well
as a legislative calendar. Operating in effect as centralized public
monopolies, these programs are organized to meet provider needs

and fight for their own survival. They thus remain fragmented, lacking strong incentives to respond to customer needs for integrated services, or to link themselves with social programs. This built-in customer insensitivity precludes any meaningful accountability as well.

Looking for new designs   It's no wonder that some state leaders have begun to question the adequacy of relying solely on the direct supplier approach. Rather than rededicate themselves to making the traditional program more effective, some state practitioners have concluded that the problem of inadequate Second Wave impact is fundamental. They have a new belief: Second Wave policies cannot be implemented successfully only by First Wave organizations. Like the U.S. automobile companies that struggled to build world-class cars with old mass-production technologies and organizations, governments cannot hope to execute Second Wave capacity-building tasks without devising new public technologies.

In the mid to late '80s, concerned policymakers cast about for new approaches. Some turned to decentralization as a way to move providers closer to their customers. Indeed, for some Second Wave efforts, like job training and technology transfer, decentralization permitted much greater customer participation in shaping services to meet particularized local needs. But while decentralization created opportunities for market feedback and even accountability, basic problems with inadequate scale and service fragmentation remained. Moreover, even when decentralized, the fact that many services were being offered by only one provider—government— preserved the programs' monopoly status, robbing them of strong incentives to change in the face of growing consumer dissatisfaction, as with the local public schools.

The Third Wave emerges

This growing awareness—that state governments must invent new organizational approaches to make Second Wave policies truly effective—has set off a "Third Wave" of experimentation in the states. The basis of the gathering Third Wave is a new realization: while government is responsible for assuring that its people and businesses have access to the resources necessary to pursue economic success, it does not have to be the sole supplier of those resources.

Scott Fosler, Vice-President of the Committee for Economic Development, describes the progression succinctly:

The transition from the first to the second wave was largely a change in policy: states expanded their focus beyond industrial recruitment to encompass the internal development of the entire state economy.

The transition from the second to the third wave, by contrast, involves important changes in organization: policy continues to focus on internal development, but new organizational approaches are used to pursue that objective.

Examples of the burgeoning state efforts to create Third Wave governance approaches abound. Most of these initiatives incorporate the decentralization pioneered to make Second Wave efforts more effective. And most move away from government as sole service provider, instead using limited government finances and authority to engage other public and private institutions in meeting development needs.

Third Wave principles   Virtually all the Third Wave initiatives are still too new for their long-term effectiveness to be assessed. Despite that, and even though they differ widely, we can now identify a set of principles around which states are constructing their Third Wave experiments.

Demand drives them   Government resources are appropriately dedicated only if what they produce is valued by the intended beneficiaries. Real demand must exist, whether it's small businesses' need for management information, manufacturers' desire for new technology, or workers' insistence on practical retraining opportunities for real jobs. Third Wave governance posits that such demand is best verified when the intended beneficiaries must invest some of their own time or resources in order to obtain the desired service.

Indiana, Michigan and Ohio recently launched manufacturing network initiatives that exemplify this. Groups of private manufacturers in these states have the primary responsibility to define their common competitive needs, like improved worker training, process modernization or new market identification. Only after sector-specific networks have defined these service needs and have themselves agreed to invest significant energy and resources in them will the state agree to invest.

They leverage resources   The Great Lakes state networks make another point. As already stated, government resources are virtually always inadequate to meet the scale of the development challenge at hand. To fully meet the true capacity demand, other institutions must dedicate their resources. Third Wave governance utilizes leverage and engagement techniques to attract private nonprofit and for-profit—as well as non-agency—public resources. This can move public agencies toward abandoning their direct supplier role in favor of approaches that encourage other organizations to commit their resources to supply the good or service in demand.

For example, Pennsylvania's Ben Franklin Partnership program funds a number of "advanced technology centers" throughout

the state, basing its dollar commitments on the financial match provided by a consortium of businesses and universities. Through the
end of FY89, $110 million in Partnership funds had been matched by
some $400 million in non-state support, including $260 million in private business contributions.

Competition is encouraged   To ensure that the essential, world-
class–quality economic resources are available and integrated to
meet customer needs, Third Wave governance relies on competition
among resource suppliers. By rejecting its old role of monopoly supplier, a government agency seeks to ensure that several private and
public providers of a needed good or service will compete for the
business. In essence, this is an extension of stating that Third Wave
initiatives seek to be customer-driven. Some Third Wave initiatives
place the actual buying power for a needed service directly in the
hands of the consumer—a practice that tends to force quality up and
price down. The Minnesota Education Choice Plan provides a good
example of where alternative suppliers—in this case, different public schools—must compete for customer loyalty and support.

They build in automatic feedback   To become accountable, Third
Wave efforts seek to build in feedback loops so automatic that they
bypass political wrangling or decisions about whether to evaluate.
This benefit follows from the customer-driven and leverage principles. If the customer defines the need and agrees to co-invest, the
line of accountability is drawn: customers' use of the service and
decisions to reinvest down the line will prove or disprove the pud-
ding. While this by itself may not ensure that all of an initiative's
public purposes are being met, if designed correctly, it can at least
establish that real demand exists among intended beneficiaries, and
that the marketplace believes the investment can earn a decent return.

The Third Wave market distinction

Organizing markets   All these principles shaping Third Wave governance—demand, leverage, competition and feedback—exist in
functioning marketplaces. Indeed, what Third Wave program approaches have in common is that they go about getting some needed
resource or service to the community by strengthening the operation of existing marketplaces, or by stimulating new ones. While
First and Second Wave programs advanced public goals by implant-
ing government as a sole supplier, Third Wave initiatives *encourage
markets to serve important public ends.*
    Third Wave initiatives seek to achieve public economic ends by
empowering the consumer beneficiaries, cultivating competitive
public *and* private suppliers, and designing new measurement, information and reward systems. If local workers need more training,

Third Wave efforts don't begin by establishing a public program to train them. Instead, the skill-deficient industries are encouraged to cooperatively define their training needs, creating effective demand. Then government can work to link the industries with private and public education service vendors who can bid for the training concession.

Public incentives may be required at the outset to induce people and institutions to think and act with each other in new ways. Those the community believes should have services, but who lack the resources to purchase them, may require subsidies to purchase services. Nonetheless, the goal is a functioning marketplace, independent of the day-to-day management by a government bureaucracy, that can provide area businesses and citizens with crucial, world-class goods and services. The same holds true whether the resource in demand is education, capital, technology transfer capacity, or growth management information.

Private markets, public purpose   However, as state and local governments increasingly employ Third Wave market-building approaches, important questions are being raised. How can government justify depending on private institutions to achieve public purposes? How can government advance critical public values such as fairness, inclusion and equity when many of its services are delivered by private organizations, some of which are motivated solely by profit? As Third Wave experiments spread across the U.S., governments are being forced to find answers to these questions.

America's economic system has long operated on the assumption that markets offer the most efficient way to produce and deliver the goods and services people want. However, even while relying on private enterprises to meet many essential needs, America has constantly reiterated the belief that markets are social creations. Their right to exist is justified by their social usefulness to the community. Well-functioning marketplaces that damage the community, such as those that produce and distribute destructive drugs or child pornography, are banned by law.

This tenet—that markets are creations of society—has served as the basic justification for citizens to work through government to regulate private markets, ensuring that their operation is consistent with public values and needs. Prescription drugs are developed and sold exclusively by private companies, but public assurance of their safety and effectiveness has been deemed essential. Therefore, the government intervenes in the operation of this marketplace by insisting that drugs receive Federal Drug Administration approval before they can be sold. Government prohibits price collusion between companies because it puts consumers at a severe disadvantage. Children's toys must meet specific safety standards or they are ordered off the shelves. The list goes on.

Vanguards of the Third Wave

Michigan Strategic Fund   The Michigan Strategic Fund (MSF) was an early effort to synthesize Second Wave policy objectives and Third Wave government approaches. Confronted with the state's innovation capital shortage, the MSF resisted setting up a direct government loan program. Instead, the MSF attempts to leverage its limited assets to create new, privately-owned financial institutions that will fill the gap, primarily with private capital.

Minnesota Choice   Third Wave experiments are not confined to straight economic development policy. Minnesota, noting the marginal improvements that educational reforms have had on public education, recognized their emphasis on centrally-directed efforts to upgrade curricula and teaching techniques. So Minnesota attempted a Third Wave approach—granting parents the "choice" to enroll their children in any public school in the state. By placing the power to choose in the hands of parent consumers, the state anticipates that the resulting competition may accomplish what traditional education reform programs have not—a world-class public school system for Minnesotans.

North Carolina Rural Economic Development Center   North Carolina found that, despite significant economic progress in its cities, many rural areas in the state were being left behind. Aware that its traditional economic development programs would never have enough dollars to help the hundreds of needy rural communities, North Carolina had a better idea. The state invested its limited resources in a non-profit, non-governmental agency, the North Carolina Rural Economic Development Center, creating an information, technical assistance and capital source that rural leaders can tap as they devise their own paths to prosperity. Rather than provide fish to every small North Carolina town and county, state leaders chose a Third Wave solution—teach the communities how to fish for themselves.

Third Wave economic development initiatives can invent equivalent mechanisms to ensure that key public values are protected and promoted. One concern is that only those with buying power will be able to secure Third Wave services, threatening the key values of participation and equity. Here, a growing number of Third Wave initiatives are working toward the provision of vouchers or other forms of purchasing power to low-income individuals or very small businesses, in order to guarantee their full participation as service consumers. Other incentives can be devised. For example, the Michigan Strategic Fund was concerned that its efforts to help form new, privately-owned, risk-capital financial institutions might not produce institutions that would serve the state's minority community. So the MSF offered special incentives to ensure that some of these new institutions would be minority-owned. In this way, the key values of broad participation and equity were promoted.

Direct supply still has its place   All this is not to suggest that there is no longer a place for direct service delivery by public economic development agencies. In many instances, public organizations are important suppliers, such as in the role the community colleges play in workforce training and some technology transfer. In Third Wave terms, the key is that they compete with other organizations, both public and private, in delivering these services.

And of course, it is critical to preserve the use of government agencies as the direct supplier of last resort. For example, if private providers are unwilling to provide quality training, financial or technical services in inner-city or remote rural areas, government must be prepared to provide them. And if a particular area can only support a single provider of some key service, that provider should either be public or, if private, closely regulated.

In short, Third Wave governance initiatives—designed to provide critical economic development resources with the scale, quality, integration and accountability needed to make a real difference in a community's economic competitiveness—require the same careful balance of private efficiency and public purpose that characterizes a successful democratic market system. Government's critical role remains as the guarantor that essential services are available and consistent with core values of fairness, full participation and equity. However, unlike traditional public service delivery, the Third Wave looks to market enhancement and market building as the initial path to effective implementation.

Reinventing government

The Third Wave is just beginning to build; we expect it will crest in the coming decade. As one might expect, the market-building activities common to Third Wave governance are forcing the engaged state and local agencies to restructure. The role of government is changing. Operating less as mass suppliers of particular goods or services, these public agencies are discovering the need to act more as facilitators, brokers and seed capitalists. As the past decade has taught many "excellent" private corporations, traditional, command-style bureaucracies cannot perform this more entrepreneurial role well. Although it's in very early stages, as the 1990s unfold, efforts to reinvent the government organization itself will surely spring up across the nation. Just as private sector organizations have had to restructure themselves to meet new global demands, so will public organizations have to adapt.

For Further Reference

Allen, David N., Jonathan Gorham, and Tripp Peake. "Small Business Incubators: Phases of Development and the Management Challenge." *Economic Development Commentary* 11, no. 2 (Summer 1987): 6–11.

Benson, Bruce L. "Do Taxes Matter?" The Impact of State and Local Taxes on Economic Development." *Economic Development Commentary* 10, no. 4 (Winter 1986): 13–17.

Beyers, William B., Michael J. Alvine, and Erik G. Johnsen. "The Service Sector: A Growing Force in the Regional Export Base." *Economic Development Commentary* 9, no. 3 (Fall 1985): 3–7.

Blakely, Edward J. "Selecting a Local Economic Development Strategy." In Edward J. Blakely, *Planning Local Economic Development*. Newbury Park, CA: Sage Publications, 1989.

Buss, Terry F., and W. Robert Kennedy. "Health, Hospitals and Economic Development: Forging a New Partnership." *Economic Development Commentary* 12, no. 2 (Summer 1988): 18–21.

Chmura, Thomas J. "The Higher Education–Economic Development Connection: Emerging Roles for Colleges and Universities." *Economic Development Commentary* 11, no. 3 (Fall 1987): 11–17.

Choate, Pat, and Juyne Linger. "Market Wars: Regaining Competitiveness in the Global Economy." *Economic Development Commentary* 10, no. 4 (Winter 1986): 8–12.

Colman, William G. "Public-Private Partnership for Community Revitalization." from William G. Colman, *State and Local Government and Public-Private Partnerships: A Policy Issues Handbook*. New York: Greenwood Press, 1989, 188–258.

Committee for Economic Development. *Children in Need: Educational Opportunities for the Disadvantaged, A Statement by the Research and Policy Committee*. New York: Committee for Economic Development, 1987.

Cook, James. "Priming the Urban Pump: A Hybrid Formula for Public Housing That May Work." *Forbes*, 23 March 1987.

Corporation For Enterprise Development. *Taken for Granted: How Grant Thornton's Business Climate Index Leads States Astray.* Washington, D.C.: Corporation for Enterprise Development, 1986.

Corporation For Enterprise Development. "Sharing Opportunities: Business Development for Low-Income People." Paper prepared for the Council of State Community Affairs Agencies, Washington, D.C., 1988.

Dewar, Margaret. "The Effectiveness of Economic Development Tools: A Review to Date." In *Financing Economic Development*, edited by Richard D. Bingham, Edward B. Hill, and Sammis B. White. Newbury Park, CA: Sage Publications, 1990.

Dodge, William R. "The Emergence of Intercommunity Partnerships in the 1980's." *Public Management* (July 1988): 2–6.

Duerksen, Christopher J. "Industrial Plant Location: Do Environmental Controls Inhibit Development?" *Economic Development Commentary* 9, no. 4 (Winter 1985): 17–21.

Eadie, Douglas C. "Strategic Issue Management: Building an Organization's Strategic Capability." *Economic Development Commentary* 11, no. 3 (Fall 1987): 18–21.

Ericson, Rodney A., Craig R. Humphrey, and Edward J. Ottensmeyer. "Nonprofit Local Industrial Development Groups: Examining Their Organization, Activities, and Effectiveness." *Economic Development Commentary* 12, no. 3 (Fall 1988): 8–12.

Feoick, Richard C. "The Adoption of Economic Development Policies by State and Local Governments: A Review." *Economic Development Quarterly* 3, no. 3 (August 1989): 266–269.

Fosler, R. Scott. "The Future Economic Role of Local Government." *Public Management* (April 1988): 3–10.

Fosler, R. Scott, "The Next Challenge in State Economic Development." *State Legislatures* (March 1989): 26.

Fosler, R. Scott, ed. *The New Economic Role of American States.* New York: Oxford University Press, 1988.

Gunyou, John. "The Municipal Development Account." *Government Finance Review* 2, no. 3 (June 1986): 7–11.

Harman, Douglas, and Ann Long Diveley. "Fort Worth Improvement District: A First in Texas." *Texas Town and City* (September 1987): 44–46.

Hatry, Harry P., et al. *Monitoring the Outcomes of Economic Development Programs.* Washington, D.C.: The Urban Institute, 1990.

Herbers, John. "North Carolina: The Prototype for America's Future." In John Herbers, *The New Heartland: America's Flight Beyond the Suburbs and How It Is Changing Our Future.* New York: Times Books, 1978, 28–38.

Hill, Edward W. "Economic Development Financing Mechanisms: An Overview." In *Financing Economic Development*, edited by Richard D. Bingham, Edward B. Hill, and Sammis B. White. Newbury Park, CA: Sage Publications, 1990.

Humphrey, Craig R., et al. "Industrial Development Groups, External Connections, and Job Generation in Local Communities." *Economic Development Quarterly* (February 1989): 32–45.

Johnson, William, and Arnold Packer. *Workforce 2000: Work and Workers for the 21st Century.* Indianapolis: The Hudson Institute and the U.S. Department of Labor, June 1987.

Kane, Matt, and Peggy Sand. "A Framework for Economic Development." In Kane and Sand, *Economic Development: What Works at the Local Level.* Washington, D.C.: National League of Cities, 1988, 10–20.

Kaplan, Marshall. "Why National Infrastructure Studies Have Failed." *The Public's Capital: A Quarterly Forum on Infrastructure Issues* 1, no. 1 (July 1989): 4.

Koppel, Jacque. "Manufacturers Must Face the Music." *High Technology* (March 1986): 12.

Lloyd, Marilyn Swartz. "Zoning in the Public Interest: Preserving Land for Job Creating." *Economic Development Commentary* 12, no. 1 (Spring 1988): 12–15.

Markusen, Ann. "High-Tech Plants and Jobs: What Really Lures Them?" *Economic Development Commentary* 10, no. 3 (Fall 1986): 3–7.

Miele, Frank. "The Canada–U.S. Freer Trade Agreement: An Economic Developer's Perspective." Paper submitted to the Committee for Economic Development, Washington, D.C., 6 January 1989, by Frank Miele, Executive Director, Economic Development Department, City of Scarborough, Ontario, Canada M1P 4N7.

National Association of Regional Councils. *State Growth Promotion and Growth Management Strategies: Utilizing Regional Councils as Key Partners.* Washington, D.C.: NARC, July 1987, 1–7.

Nothdurft, William E. "Marketing Policy." *Entrepreneurial Economy Review* (Winter 1988).

Nothdurft, William E. "Schoolworks." In William E. Nothdurft, *Schoolworks: Reinventing Public Schools to Create the Workforce of the Future.* Washington, D.C.: The German Marshall Fund of the United States and The Brookings Institution, 1989.

Osborne, David. *Laboratories of Democracy.* Boston: Harvard Business School Press, 289–291, 300–315.

Pilcher, Dan. "Economic Development: Old Term Has New Meaning." *State Legislatures* (August 1986): 18.

Plosila, Walter H. "State Technical Development Programs." *Forum for Applied Research and Public Policy* (Summer 1987): 30–38.

Quinn-Campbell, Kathleen, Will McWhinney, and Alan Tandy. "Community Consensus to Economic Development." Paper submitted to the Committee for Economic Development, Washington, D.C., 2 February 1989. Article can be obtained from Alan Tandy, City Administrator, City of Billings, P. O. Box 1178, Billings, MT.

Rosenthal, Warren, and Michelle Burkett. "An Analysis of Rural Economic Development." *County News* 24 October 1988.

Storper, Michael, and Susan Christopherson. "Flexible Specialization and Regional Industrial Agglomerations: The Case of the U.S. Motion Picture Industry." *Annals of the Association of American Geographers* 77, no. 1 (1987): 104–117.

Summers, Anita A., and Thomas F. Luce. "Economic Development within the Philadelphia Metropolitan Area." Philadelphia: University of Pennsylvania Press, 1987, 1–8.

Swager, Ronald J. "The Targeting Study in Economic Development Practice." *Economic Development Review* (Summer 1987) 56–60.

Voinivich, George V. "A Blueprint for America's Cities: Fostering Effective Public-Private Part-nerships." *Economic Development Commentary* 11, no. 2 (Summer 1987): 3–5.

Wolkoff, Michael. "The Effectiveness of Economic Development Tools: A State and Local Perspective." In *Financing Economic Development*, edited by Richard D. Bingham, Edward B. Hill, and Sammis B. White. Newbury Park, CA: Sage Publications, 1990.

Practical Management Series

Local Economic Development: Strategies for a Changing Economy

Text type
Century Expanded

Composition
Graphic Composition, Inc.
Athens, Georgia

Printing and binding
R. R. Donnelley & Sons Company
Harrisonburg, Virginia

Cover design
Rebecca Geanaros